ANOTHER LUCKY GUY
WITH ALS

Michal Slezák

Foreword and Afterword
by Darren Baker

Handshake Press

ISBN 978-1-7392249-8-1

*To my beloved wife and children
Kamča, Olda, Vincent, Hubert*

FOREWORD

In 1992, I arrived in Czechoslovakia to teach English in a high school. The next year the country split in half and I found myself in the Czech Republic twenty miles from the new border with Slovakia. I had several hundred students, most of them studying English as their main foreign language. Some joined me in extracurricular activities after school like learning how to play baseball and that "other" football.

One student who took part in these activities was not from our school. He was friends with some of the others and had tagged along because he was outgoing and liked to try new things. I could tell that because he had a skateboard, which you saw very few of at that time. His name was Michal Slezák, probably the twentieth Michal I had met there so far.

Years passed. I married a local girl, settled down, and left the school system. Once in a while I would run into a former student who updated me on what the others were doing. I learned that Michal had spent several years in America and one in Australia as a snowboard instructor. Apparently, he had taken that skateboard to a whole new level.

Decades passed. One day my son, who became an English and history teacher in high school, told me that the father of one of his students remembered me as that guy who taught him how to play baseball. This was Michal, and we got re-acquainted online, where I could see he was living quite the life with his family and friends. During our exchange of messages, he revealed he had MND.

I was stunned. MND stands for Motor Neuron Disease, the British term for Amyotrophic Lateral Sclerosis, or ALS. I have known what ALS is ever since I watched the 1942 movie *The Pride of the Yankees*, the story of baseball player Lou Gehrig, who died of the disease in 1941.

Some weeks later, Michal posted an appeal for funds to help pay off his mortgage. That gave me an idea and we met to discuss it. It had been nearly thirty years since I last saw him, when he was a teenager. He was the same as I remembered him. Tall, gangly, always chipper. He had already lost the use of his left arm and hand, and he drank through a straw. We talked about the time we played baseball on the grassy lot where a retirement home now stands.

Given all his travels, I suggested that Michal write a book about his life. I figured his experience in America and overall adventures, concluding with his search for a treatment for ALS, made an inspiring story. By publishing it, he would have a product to sell and raise the money he needs that way.

He talked it over with his wife and it was agreed. Over the course of two months, we met to talk about his life. Although ALS remains an elusive disease, with no known cause or cure, Michal is determined to beat it by exploring numerous physical and spiritual therapies. Something is obviously working, because it's already been four years since his diagnosis and yet he looks and feels relatively healthy and optimistic.

The title of the book comes from the speech Gehrig gave after ALS cut his career short. He said he had caught a bad break, but considered himself lucky for the life he had been given. ALS made him aware of just how much he still had to live for. So it is with Michal, as you hear him tell his story here in his own words.

KEY TO CZECH PRONUNCIATION

é – b**e**d	ž – trea**s**ure
ě – **y**et	ý – gr**i**t
j – **y**et	á – sp**a**
č – **ch**urch	í – fr**ee**
c – pi**zz**a	ř – roll an **r** on the back
š – **s**ure	of your front teeth

I WAS BORN ON February 9, 1977, in Frýdek-Místek, a city of about 60,000 people. I share the same birthday as my father, Jiří, who was born thirty-three years before me in Ostrava, the largest city in North Moravia. Ostrava lies twenty miles north of Frýdek-Místek and has a population five times bigger.

Coalmining turned this entire region into an industrial powerhouse, which the Germans exploited to manufacture arms for the Wehrmacht during their wartime occupation. My grandparents had two children in that time and added a third after the war ended. I never knew either of them. My grandmother died of cancer in her fifties, and my grandfather, who was a teetotaler, died of cirrhosis of the liver brought on by hepatitis.

I hardly got to know my father's two brothers. The oldest one, Pavel, fled the country after the Russians and their allies occupied Czechoslovakia in 1968. Actually, he didn't flee. The border was opened up for a certain period of time to allow discontented Czechs and Slovaks to leave on their own. Thousands took advantage of it, knowing however that they could never come back.

Pavel, his wife, and stepdaughter first went to Sweden, lived there for several years, then to West Germany, lived there for several years, and finally ended up in Canada. I met them for the first time when they visited after the fall of the communist regime in 1989. My other uncle Karel settled in South Moravia with his family. He became politically active for a spell and rose to become vice-mayor of the city where he lives now.

All this stuff you hear about middle children growing up with hang-ups; that wasn't my father. He was always easy-going, always helpful, always ready with a good story to tell. Like his brothers, he was trained in the engineering field, but he was the only one of them to work for the state mining company.

It was a good move professionally. In those days, miners were like gods. They did the hard, dangerous work that kept the lights on and the water hot, and they were rewarded for it. They jumped to the head of the line for housing and expensive commodities like cars and bikes. They got early retirement, and their salaries were typically higher than college-educated workers.

Some miners didn't wash the coal dust out of their eyelashes after work. They walked around with it like they were wearing mascara. That way, people who saw them knew that they were a cut above them and everybody else.

My father never worked down below. He got a position in the surface processing plant, which spared his health while entitling him to the same benefits enjoyed by the miners who went down and dug. He soon showed he had a knack for making things better and racked up scores of improvements in his career.

For example, the sludge created from washing coal was sent to a settling tank. After drying, the residue was sold for next to nothing to homeowners, who burned it in their chimneys and furnaces. The smoke from it was pollution at its worst. It could be seen and smelled for miles around.

My father proposed installing a filter press in the sludge line to separate the solids from the liquid. Since the solids were basically washed coal, they could be sold at the price of coal itself. This not only generated a profit where there had been none before, but it was better for the environment.

Improvements like that earned my father recognition and bonuses. His future looked bright, but my uncle Pavel's choice of capitalism over communism hung over my father's advancement in the mining company. The easiest way to get around it was to join the communist party, which he eventually did.

It was a cynical career move, but it worked. My father rose to become a plant boss in charge of two hundred people. It also helped that he improved himself by obtaining a university degree through correspondence study. He began it just after I was born, but the combination of work during the week and study on the weekend meant I have very few memories of him before I started school.

He was already a divorced father of a young girl when one day he picked up the young woman who became my mother. He saw her hitchhiking and gave her a lift to the workers' hostel where she was living at the time. My mother was born Helena Kundratová in Zábřeh na Moravě, a small town about eighty miles to the west on the border with Bohemia. She never knew the eldest of her three brothers because he died of a bronchial infection when he was eleven.

My grandmother was forty-two years old when my mother was born in 1950, so my grandparents were well into their seventies when I saw them for the first time. I absolutely adored them. My grandfather was a classicist who taught Latin and Greek in high school until he was fired for criticizing the Russian-led invasion. I fondly remember our walks around town while my grandmother baked all kinds of delicious cakes and snacks for our return.

Despite smoking forty cigarettes a day, my grandfather was a dedicated mountain climber and passed on his skills and enthusiasm to his sons. The second oldest, my uncle Arnošt, got a spot on the Czech expedition that climbed the 24,500-foot Mount Nun in the Himalayas in October 1976, just a few months before I was born. They not only pioneered a new route to the top, but all eight members of the climbing team reached the summit. It was a great success, but Arnošt, who can be seen below sitting third from the left, ended up losing two toes to frostbite.

My other uncle, named Pavel like the émigré uncle on my father's side, is my godfather. The first time I went to the top of Lysá hora, the tallest mountain in the Beskydy range, it was under his guidance. I was ten at the time and it began my lifelong passion with the mountains that cover our corner of North Moravia. Both Pavel the émigré and Arnošt the mountain climber married women named Věra, as did my father's youngest brother Karel, so I had a total of three Aunt Věras.

My mother never got into climbing like her brothers. Her sport was track and field and she got to be so good in the high jump and long jump that her coach forbade her to learn skiing like the rest of the students in her school. He was worried she would break a leg or twist an ankle and that would be the end of her jumping.

My father was a passionate skier and figured he would teach her after they got married. He even gave her ski gloves during their first Christmas together as an incentive, but no dice. As far as she was concerned, that ship had sailed. Whenever our family went skiing, she got used to waiting in a nearby establishment with a book and coffee or grog until we were done for the day.

One thing he did turn my mother on to was rally racing. It was a popular sport in the 1970s, with ordinary people entering their family cars in these tests of timing and navigation on open roads. My father drove while my mother acted as his navigator, warning him of upcoming turns or pointing them out as they appeared. Given that they met in the front seat of his car, and hit it off there, it seemed like a fitting hobby for the two of them to enjoy, but they gave it up after they settled into family life together. By no means, however, did that put an end to her telling him how to drive.

Their first and only home is a nice, relatively spacious two-bedroom apartment in Frýdek-Místek. My brother Jenda was born first and I came along three and a half years later. As a whole, I can say my memories of childhood are happy and endearing. A lot of that feeling is connected to all the traveling we did.

Here again, my father's decision to join the communist party paid off, because the families of émigrés were generally never allowed to go abroad, not even to other countries behind the Iron Curtain. By showing his loyalty to the system, my father made it possible for us to travel to the seaside of Yugoslavia, which is a big thing when you live in a landlocked country.

But you needed more than just permission to travel abroad. You also needed money and most jobs didn't pay enough money for people to take fancy vacations. They had to settle for vacations in the mountains or at the lakeside subsidized by their places of employment. We didn't have this problem thanks to the money my father earned from his improvements at work. We even flew once, in a Russian-made airliner, to a Black Sea resort in Bulgaria.

The trips by car were anything but comfortable. The countries of eastern Europe had no highway network in those days, so we plodded along on two-lane roads, some not in very good condition, and often struggled to get around a truck or tractor. Our car was small and had no headrest in the backseat, so my brother and I constantly squirmed for position. We passed the time by reading comics and books, playing games like word train, or just staring out the window at the landscape. At night, we stuffed our travel bags into the footholds so my brother and I could sleep side by side across the seat.

Our best vacation was in Croatia. We lived in a house for a full twenty-three days close to the shoreline. Every day it was sunshine and ice cream and swimming in the warm, crystal-clear Adriatic Sea. We stumbled on a nudist beach during one of our jaunts. Was that ever an eye-opener for a thirteen-year-old! We visited the beautiful historic cities of Dubrovnik and Mostar, never realizing that within a couple of years they would suffer considerable damage in the Balkan wars of independence that broke out in the 1990s.

Outside of vacation, most of our summers were spent at the cottage my parents bought just after I was born. It was located thirty-five miles southwest in the countryside of Wallachia. The cottage was actually an old house made of unfired bricks, and since the walls had begun to sag, my parents decided to build a real cottage made of wood inside the old one. The project is still ongoing today.

The building works aside, I loved these weekends. We had a forest behind us in which there were several meadows. We went exploring, played games, picked mushrooms and berries, in general loved the wide-open space and fresh air that you appreciate when you grow up in an apartment complex. The only real amenity missing was an indoor toilet. We had to trek to the outhouse located a hundred yards away. I can't say it's the most pleasant experience in the world, particularly in the middle of the night, but you get used to it.

These were the times when my brother and I were the closest, but once we reached school age, the differences between us were clear. He never went in for sports besides skiing and snowboarding. He's a technical type who always did brilliant in school. He later became what we might call a classic IT guy.

When it came time for me to focus my high school education, I was told that I had an aptitude for numbers. I should become either an economist or teacher. My choice of high schools was Petr Bezruč, named after a famous local poet. It was the best in the city for those who wanted to go on to university. I aced my entrance exam, mostly through luck, I suspect, and was admitted.

High school was the best of times. The teachers were all cool and they treated us with dignity and respect. I noticed girls for the first time and they noticed me because I was tall and slim. I also noticed that the more sports you did, the less time you spent in class. So I did soccer, swimming, volleyball and track.

I also did gymnastics. I learned the horizontal bar, how to jump over the vault and do flips in the floor exercise. I started the rings in my second year, but ultimately, I didn't have the strength for them. Our coach, who was also our civics teacher, twice led our team to victory in the national championships.

It was just after I started high school that I noticed this kid riding around on a skateboard. I found out who he was and knocked on his door. I told him I wanted to buy a skateboard and learn to ride it. His name was Mirek, and a week later he went with me to Olomouc, a historic city sixty miles to the west. It had one of the few shops that sold skateboards at that time. The one I bought cost 5,000 Czech crowns, or about $125 at the exchange rate in those days. It was equal to the monthly salary of a new teacher.

I had the money from all the odd jobs I was doing. I helped out at the swimming pool, cleaned windows, assembled office furniture. I got on average a buck an hour. My parents were resigned to me getting a skateboard. They knew I jumped at any new sport that came my way. Plus, they felt guilty because, back in middle school, they promised to buy me a good tennis racket to replace the crappy one that I had, but they reneged on it.

But the money I spent didn't stop at 5,000 crowns. The whole point of the skateboard was to do tricks, and that inevitably led me to breaking the deck on the board no less than on twenty-six separate occasions. Since each deck cost around 2,000 crowns ($50), I ended up shelling out an extra ten times what I paid for the skateboard.

I ended up on my ass plenty of times, to be sure. The worst accident occurred when I attempted to jump over a concrete stairway of ten steps. Not until I reached the top edge of the stairway did I realize it wasn't a good idea, but it was too late. I tumbled down the steps hard. I slowly got up and noticed that my left forearm just dangled there.

I had dislocated my elbow. It didn't really hurt, so I thought nothing of pushing the bone back into the joint, but the second it snapped in place, that's when the pain started. It got so unbearable that I threw up, though not on the steps, thank god. Later, I went to a doctor to have it checked out and she doubted I had actually dislocated it. It would be the worst pain imaginable, she informed me.

Today, I have lots of good friends, but in my youth, it was always just a single friend during a single period, a best friend if you will, and in my high school years it was Mirek.

He went to a different school, one that trained students for the hospitality industry, and he was always cutting class to go skateboarding. Naturally, he wanted me to join him. Several times he appeared outside the window of my classroom. With the help of my classmates, I was able to jump through the window when the teacher's back was turned. As far as I know, my presence was never missed.

Snowboarding seemed like the next logical step. It was an easy transition because I was a lousy skier. For some reason, my father never taught me to ski like he did my brother, who was really good at it, but Jenda switched to snowboarding when the opportunity came. Snowboards were even harder to come by than skateboards, but he had a friend who made them by hand. This guy made one for me too, free of charge because he just liked to make them.

He heated up a piece of plywood to create the bend of the nose and tail, applied a coating of plastic and wax to the bottom to make it slippery, and added metal trim around the edges. He then took the bindings from my skis and screwed them into the wood. I still can't believe I did my first snowboarding with ski boots on. It was awkward as hell and on the third day I broke the bindings. That ended that experiment.

Since Mirek had a new snowboard, I bought his old one despite knowing there were two obvious problems. First, he's much shorter than me, so his board was really short. And second, he leads with his right foot on the nose, whereas I lead with my left. To make it work, I had to swap his bindings for my own, which meant removing the eight screws that attached each binding to the board, filling in the holes with an epoxy compound, and screwing on the new bindings. There were thirty-two holes in that one board.

These were truly the early days of snowboarding. There was no special shoes or clothing, just whatever you had on. I snowboarded in my jeans and regular winter jacket. On the slopes you might find two snowboarders for every hundred skiers, who typically resented our presence, but that was mostly because we always tried to cut in line. We thought it was the cool thing to do, so we did it.

When I was a junior, forty students from my school plus three teachers boarded a bus for Holland. There was an exchange program set up between our school and another one not far from Amsterdam. It was my first trip without my parents, and while it was a tight fit for the 750 miles we covered, I had a blast. I had my skateboard with me and Holland was full of skate parks.

We stayed with families who were really nice to us. We went bowling, ate endless amounts of pizza, all of it terribly expensive. The North Sea was quite cold in June, but it didn't stop me or my classmate Hynek from jumping in. Another classmate got wasted on Dutch beer, then tried to ride a bike and went face first into the pavement. He came home with three broken front teeth.

As high school was coming to an end, I ditched any thought of becoming a teacher and decided to study economics at the university. My motivation was money. Commercial television had arrived in our country from America. We saw families living in big houses with swimming pools, and high school kids driving expensive cars and hanging out at the mall.

We had neither cars nor malls, much less the credit cards all those kids seemed to have. The big thing we did here after school was grab a hot dog and hang out in the park or by the river. Cheap, simple, and the best of times.

2

MONEY WAS THE NORMAL GIFT to high-schoolers upon graduation. The generation before us used their money to furnish their future homes and could not understand how our generation wanted to use it for traveling. The only trip they were willing to give us was a guilt trip. I decided back in Holland that I was going to see something of the world before entering my first furniture store, but my mother is nothing if not persistent. I chose to play it safe and put the money that my parents gave me in the bank. I passed the admissions exam for the Mining and Technical University of Ostrava and enrolled there for the following autumn.

My freshman year was a disaster. I tried out for the basketball team, but didn't make the cut. The swimming team took me, but I dropped out when it was clear I was out of my league. Worst of all, I failed my mid-terms and finals in Math, normally my best subject. The problem was, my math class started at 7:15 in the morning. To get there, I had to take the 6:05 train to Ostrava. Once I reached the big hall where the class was held, I flopped into a seat and snoozed until the end.

Fortunately, shirkers like me were given one more chance to take the final exam again in August. I spent the whole summer studying and nailed it. My teacher was surprised at just how well I did and was almost apologetic for the fact that, given my two earlier failures, she could only give me a "C" for the year, but that was fine with me.

After that, I carefully manipulated my schedule so that I had to go to school for only two days during the week. The other three days I worked to make money. My main source was cleaning windows for seniors who lived in apartment complexes. The windows in these buildings were large and had to be unscrewed in order to clean between the double glazing. The hour I needed for each window earned me a hundred crowns, or two and a half bucks. And then, midway through my seventh semester of the five-year program, I got an offer to make some real money.

There was lots of real money to be made at that time. The Czech economy was referred to as the Wild East because the post-totalitarian government, which took liberal democracy as its model, decided to go from communism to capitalism overnight. All state-owned industries, practically the entire economy, were turned into publicly-traded companies.

Adult citizens were invited to buy shares in them with a book of vouchers given to them by the government. And just like that, the working class was transformed into investors without any understanding of a market economy. Clever, politically-connected entrepreneurs bought up enough shares to become the owners of huge factories.

That's what happened to the state mining company. It came under control of a single owner, which seemed like his bad luck, because the mines were obsolete and could not hope to compete in a free market. But the new owner wasn't interested in saving them. The sooner he stripped them of their assets, the better.

What he really wanted were the thousands of apartments that had been built for the mining company to dole out to its workers. According to the privatization agreement he had with the government, he was supposed to sell those apartments to the people living in them. He reneged on it, got away with it, and today he keeps raising the rent for his thousands of tenants, including my parents. It's swindles like these that led some members of the older generation to refer to communism as a golden age.

Not being old enough at the time, I had to miss out on the vouchers, but I got my chance to play the market when a couple of finance students approached me to start a branch office for a new brokerage firm in Prague. We got the license and software and went to work building up a client base of unskilled investors. Basically, we recommended certain commodities to them, placed their orders after they put up 10% of the value, and got a commission for each trade. It was just like on Wall Street, and I loved it.

I hadn't forgotten about my dream to travel. In the summer of 1997, I walked into a travel agency with my girlfriend Lenka to see if they had any last-minute trips abroad. They had a bus going to Greece for fourteen days, travel included, for just $75 each. The catch was, it was leaving in a few hours. We raced home, collected the money, packed a few bags, and off we went.

It took us two days to get to the campsite located just south of Mount Olympus. We were given a large tent that was partitioned off for two couples. We zipped up for the night on one side, the other couple zipped up on the other. We were right next to the Aegean Sea, maybe ten yards from it at the most, and the sound of the waves put us to sleep straightaway.

For sightseeing, we got around by hitchhiking. First, it was 120 miles north to Thessaloniki, then 240 miles south to Athens. For Athens, our plan was to hitchhike through the night and arrive there in the morning. We got a ride in a minivan with a Romanian family. Unfortunately, their destination was eleven miles short of the city and it was already after midnight when their exit approached. We had no choice but to get out on the highway.

As might be expected, not a single car stopped for us. We had to walk on the shoulder the whole time, cars screaming by us in the dark, but what was really scary were the packs of feral dogs we encountered. They were everywhere and none too friendly. After hours of walking, we found a bus stop and a driver who told us that he was going to the center. It turned out he meant the center of a suburb on the outskirts of Athens.

There was a subway station just a few hundred yards away. We hopped on and got off at the station close to the Acropolis. It was 6:30 in the morning and very few people were there. We practically had the entire temple to ourselves. In the evening, we hitchhiked back and got a ride with a trucker. Half of the guy's face was horribly swollen because, the day before, a bird flew in through his side-door window. It shattered the glass and smacked him in the face. He still wasn't over the shock of it.

We found that communication with him and other older Greeks was helped by the connection between Greece and Czechoslovakia in the postwar years, when our country gave refuge to many Greek communists fleeing the CIA-backed government in Athens. Some still remembered a few words of our language. When they learned that we were Czech, they couldn't express their gratitude enough for the help they and their families received. The family of this truck driver was one of them. He drove us all the way to our campsite in the north.

The next summer, in 1998, we went camping in South Bohemia. As we walked over Zvíkovský Bridge, which spans the Vltava River from a height of 250 feet, I noticed some bungee jumping going on. I was curious and told Lenka that I was just going to find out how it worked, how much it cost, and so forth. Just get information, nothing more.

When she arrived minutes later, I was in a harness, ready to take a leap of faith. She told me I was nuts and walked away. It was certainly a thrilling experience, but it flew by in a flash and, when I came to think about it later on, not really worth the trust I put in some total strangers to make sure I was safe.

My next chance to travel abroad came the following year in 1999. That summer, Lenka was one of the organizers of an international folk festival hosted by our city. She enlisted my aid as a translator for some of the groups, and it was in this capacity that I got to know Mustafa in the Turkish group. He insisted that we visit his country, so in August, we boarded a bus for the two-day ride to Istanbul.

I was making money then, but I still needed some of my furniture money for the trip. My mother was unhappy about it, not just about the money, but about traveling in general. She said she didn't see the point of it. Of course, that was nonsense. We traveled a lot when I was a kid. She just couldn't admit that she wished she had had the same opportunities for work and travel when she was young and ready to take on the world.

Mustafa met us in Istanbul and took us straight away to Ankara, the modern capital where he lived with his family. In all, we spent the next three weeks traveling around with various members of his family. Cappadocia in the heartland was absolutely amazing. It's a very historic site with cone-shaped houses and a dry, rugged landscape full of chimney rocks. We went to Pamukkale, famous for hot springs of crystal-clear water in limestone cascading down the mountainside. Wading in those pools was an experience for a lifetime.

Both Cappadocia and Pamukkale are famous tourist sites. The nice thing about traveling with a Turkish family is they know the places not on the map. At one point, they turned onto a dirt road with no signs that went on for mile after mile. Finally, we arrived at a campsite overlooking the Aegean Sea. The view was as breathtaking as we could have hoped for, and there were only Turkish people there. It was an unforgettable night of good food and drink and the music and dance of the country.

One thing about the food, though. On the way to Turkey, I read a guide book that warned travelers not to buy any food from street vendors. When we got off the bus in Istanbul, we couldn't resist the kebab being sold at a stand on the corner. It was great and so were all the other kebabs we bought from street vendors throughout our time there. No problems at all. Then we stayed a night at a hotel, went to the breakfast buffet the next morning, and puked our guts out for the rest of the day.

Bodrun on the Aegean coast is another historic city, the site of Halicarnassus made famous by Herodotus. Here, we rented a car, went to Izmir, and from there to Istanbul. We didn't realize until later on that we totally missed Troy. I can't remember if we knew it was there or not, but on the way to Istanbul, we saw the destruction of the earthquake that hit Turkey the day after we reached Ankara. We were preoccupied with getting home. Our outbound bus was unaffected by the emergency and we were home in two days.

Like many people returning from a great vacation, we already made plans to go back. In fact, we planned to go even further to Syria after talking to some Czech travelers on the bus to Turkey who were going on to Damascus. We figured we would do the same next time, but it never happened. When I went to Turkey next, in 2018, Damascus had been destroyed by war.

Lenka spent the next winter semester studying at the university of Jönköping in Sweden along with two Czech girlfriends. They were coming home in June 2000 and I offered to drive there for them. I got in my blue Škoda 130 and drove the length of Poland to catch a ferry across the Baltic Sea.

The border control at the Polish port noticed that the picture in my passport was becoming unglued at the edge. Thousands of Czech passports had this defect. They warned me that the Swedes might give me a hard time about it. I took my chances and ended up waiting for four hours in my car after arriving in Malmö. At first, I didn't know why, because no one told me anything.

The problem was my passport picture all right, but not

because it was becoming unglued, rather it showed me with long curly hair, not the buzz-cut I foolishly got before leaving. The border officials called the number I provided to verify my identity. My brother Jenda answered the phone. He confirmed that he had a brother with my name, but when asked where that brother was, he answered, "He went somewhere." Just somewhere, as if he had no clue I might be in an entirely different country at the moment.

In the end, they let me in. It had been a real pain in the ass, but worth it because, before I left, Lenka warned me not to bring any alcohol or food into the country. It was strictly forbidden. Of course, we were planning to do some traveling, and Sweden is terribly expensive, so I hid away lots of supplies. In all the ruckus about my passport, they never thought to search my car for contraband.

I drove the 180 miles from Malmö to Jönköping and picked the girls up there. We went up to see Stockholm, and on the way back, I got a flat tire. It was actually blown out at the side, probably the consequence of having four people in a car stuffed full of bags, with one huge one outside tied to the roof.

I had to dig out a lot of stuff to get to the spare tire, only to find that it was flat as well. I walked up to a house next to the highway and the people inside went out of their way to help us find a tire service, which wasn't easy because it was a state holiday. After an hour, a mechanic arrived with a new tire. It looked beautiful and smelled nice, but the total cost was $130, which could buy four new tires in the Czech Republic. I prayed the other three tires held out, because all I had left after that was gas money.

Back home, I threw myself into my final year of study and work as a stockbroker. One day I got the brilliant idea to get in on the action myself. I went to a bank to borrow 200,000 crowns, which was roughly equal to $5,000. I was a college student with no savings, no collateral, and nobody to co-sign for me. The bank approved my loan. It was one of the many private banks and credit unions that were popping up at that time to gamble on hitting the jackpot like everybody else. Nearly all them failed in the next few years, including mine.

I invested the money in oats. To this day, I don't know why I chose oats, but it drove me nuts checking the charts to see how they were doing. They were up, they were down, sometimes they did nothing at all. The only break in my vigilance occurred after I sprained my ankle in a game of pickup basketball. I was unable to get to the office in Ostrava and my home computer didn't have remote access to our trading system.

Finally, after three days, I showed up, lit up the screen, and there it was. Nothing. All my oats were gone. My entire investment had been wiped out, just like that. What's more, it coincided with our decision to close the office. We made some money playing stock brokers, but poured it back into advertising and rental fees and were lucky to break even.

In 2001, I graduated from the university with my degree in economics. I was twenty-four years old, living at home, with no job or good prospects, and I had this massive debt hanging over me of which my parents knew nothing.

But I had a way out already set up. I met up with a friend from the neighborhood, Michal Štefek, who was then living and working in America. When I told him about my problem, he asked what I was waiting for. The exchange rate between dollars and crowns meant that I could pay off my debt much sooner doing a crappy job in America than with a regular job here at home. You just have to live a frugal lifestyle there, he said, which wasn't too hard coming from our background.

All through school and growing up, all we ever heard about was America. Lots of my friends wanted to go there, to travel around and experience the lifestyle, but I never had that desire. Now I saw it as the answer to my problem. Lenka and I talked about it and decided to go for it.

3

IT WAS RELATIVELY EASY to get to America in the nineties. Working there was an entirely different matter. You were not allowed to work there legally, and if you got caught trying to do so, they deported your ass and wouldn't let you back in for five years. An exception was made for students, who were welcome to come over and do unskilled work for minimum wage. Since I was technically a student until the end of summer, I sent an application to an agency and they went to work on getting me a visa for this purpose.

Where and what to do in America was the big thing. Lenka and I wanted to be in the mountains, and from the long list of options available, we chose Sun Valley, Idaho. We knew nothing about it, but the name was irresistible. I applied for the job of chair lift operator, because I wanted to be outdoors, and Lenka was going to work in a store that made boxed candies out of chocolate.

The first thing we did was find Idaho on the map. It's typical of Europeans to laugh at Americans for their poor geography skills, but it's the same for us when it comes to the states of America. Even the excuse you hear over here, that "at least I can find the United States on the map" seems lame and smug when you consider that the Czech Republic is smaller than the state of South Carolina, which itself is pretty small compared to other states.

With our location set, we talked to an employee at the agency to work out our journey there. The first stop was

New York, where we had to attend an introductory meeting for all students coming to America to work, and from there we would fly to Salt Lake City, rent a car, and drive the four hours it took to get to Sun Valley.

THE WORLD

Since I had to borrow more money to pay for the services of the agency, I sold my car at the bazaar to pay for my plane ticket. It wasn't an easy thing to do. My parents had given it to me after they bought a new one. I took the money to the agency, only to learn that airfares had tripled in price. That left us with only enough money to fly to New York. We would have to hop on a Greyhound bus for the trip across country.

There was no great emotional sendoff with friends or family before we boarded the train to Prague for our flight from the airport there. Back in the nineties, Prague was a glorious city with enviable charm. My friends and I had always taken every opportunity to go there just to hang out.

I suppose the same could be said about New York when we arrived there in June 2001. We absolutely loved it, the bustle, the smells, the action on every corner. We were put up in a dormitory at New York University, where we attended the mandatory lecture on life and culture in the U.S. We were told what to do, what not to do, and how to get a social security number, which was essential for our jobs.

The afternoon was free, so we looked around and ended up at the World Trade Center. We walked in, then walked right back out. We couldn't afford the ticket to the top. Since we would be passing through New York on our way home, with lots of money, we hoped, we could try it then. Little did we or anyone else realize.

The trip to Idaho took three days. We changed buses in Chicago, which gave us a couple of hours to look around before the next leg of our journey began. All we managed to see was Cermak Road, which was named after Anton Cermak, a Czech immigrant who became mayor in 1931 but was assassinated two years later in the company of President Roosevelt. This particular road was named after him because it ran through several Czech neighborhoods that existed there at that time.

After Chicago, we could see the landscape start to open up. We also got a good lesson in the toughness of rules in America. Every now and then the bus stopped at a gas station to let the driver and passengers stretch, use the bathroom, get a drink, and so on. At a gas station in the middle of nowhere, the driver told us we were leaving ten past ten, no ifs, ands or buts. When one of the passengers failed to show up, he walked down the aisle, grabbed the man's backpack, and threw it off the bus. He then closed the door and left.

The end of the line was Twin Falls, Idaho. We left the Greyhound and got on a regional bus that took us 85 miles north to Sun Valley. We could instantly see there was nothing normal about this place. I had read that it was a playground for the superrich and famous from all over the world, but the first thing I noticed stepping off the bus were all the cracks in the sidewalks and the potholes in the street. The hotel, lodge, condos, everything looked a bit tired.

But there they were, the oligarchs, celebrities, bodyguards, limousines. All that wealth stood in contrast to the Mormonism that seemingly dominated the spirit of the place. It certainly dominated the rules that governed us, or at least our employer wanted it to look that way. We were forbidden to drink any alcohol, and getting caught in the dormitory of the opposite sex after ten o'clock at night could get you deported. A few rooms were allotted to couples, and Lenka and I were fortunate to snag one of these.

The dormitories looked like lodges on the outside, but inside they were your typical college residences, with very small rooms for two or three people. The food in the cafeteria was excellent. A wide variety of dishes, all very cheap. At seven in the morning, after a hearty breakfast of scrambled eggs, hash browns, bacon and French toast, I took a bus to Bald Mountain and the chairlift stations.

There were two lifts running in summertime, each with two people working at the bottom station and two at the top. I was assigned to the upper station, which was perched about a mile below the top of the mountain. Usually visitors exited the lift, walked to the top and back, had lunch at the restaurant next to the station, then headed back down on one of the chairs.

My job was simple. I was to make sure people got seated in the moving chair without mishap. On my very first day, I learned that the only real problem was when groups of people tried to squeeze in more than the four persons allowed per chair. I didn't understand the point of it. A party of five could easily go three in one chair and two in the next one, but in Sun Valley, for some reason, there were always people breaking the rule and we had to intervene, sometimes even stopping the lift.

It was often rich college kids, but even the high and mighty did it. The most unpleasant situation I had to deal with occurred when Arnold Schwarzenegger appeared with four other people to take the lift downhill. I could see they had a squeeze on their mind, so I walked up and politely asked them to divide into two groups. Schwarzenegger told me not to worry about, that his niece would ride on his lap going down.

I reminded him what the rule was, but he ignored me and led the others to the spot where the chair would pick them up. So I went into the station cabin and hit the stop button. He got all pissed off and demanded to see my supervisor, who came out and told him the same thing I told him. No more than four people in the chair, dude.

Schwarzenegger finally backed down, but not before mumbling at us under his breath. I don't know how often he plays pricks on the screen, but he sure knows how to be one in real life. His temper tantrum might have been forgivable if, when getting seated on the chair, he looked at me and growled, "I'll be back," but he wasn't about to give this punk any satisfaction.

Happily, other celebrities were very courteous. Once I saw Clint Eastwood and his wife Dina and couldn't resist going up to say hello. They had to be tired of people approaching them in this manner, but they smiled and he even pulled me in close for a handshake. Later, after I became a snowboard instructor there, I taught the niece of Jodie Foster. I didn't know her name when we came into contact, but I instantly recognized her from *The Silence of the Lambs*. She too was nice and pleasant the whole time on the mountain.

I worked forty hours a week on the mountain at $6.50 an hour. It wasn't much, so I went in search of jobs to do after my shift and on weekends. I went to nearby Ketchum, famous as the place where Hemingway shot himself, and started asking the storeowners if they had something for me. I got lucky with this guy from South Africa.

He fell in love with Sun Valley after coming there to work like me. Seeing how rich people liked to buy art on vacation, he returned with a bunch of it from Africa and opened a small gallery. He paid me a dismal wage to mind the store while he did other stuff, but the money was in cash and he was an easy guy to work for.

I also sold printed t-shirts, waited at banquets, washed dishes in a restaurant, and baked pizza, including the free one I got to take home. In that one season alone, I earned enough money to pay off all my debts. I applied to come back and work during the winter season, not just for the money but also the snowboarding.

Lenka, however, had been less thrilled with Sun Valley and decided she wasn't going back. She wasn't big on winter sports and didn't care for the life we had there, which really wasn't any life when you consider I had only two days off in the five months we were there.

Before returning home, we took the opportunity of being in America to visit Mexico. We were warned that traveling by bus there carried the risk of getting robbed by the cartels, but there was never a hint of that happening. The only dangerous situation we encountered happened at this town where the bus station was quite far from the city center. We hitchhiked and were picked up by two guys who asked us to join them for a beer.

We agreed and paid for their beer, but then they asked for more money. Their tone escalated to the point where we had to run for it, and I mean literally run for it, because they started chasing us. By good fortune we ran in the direction of the local hotel. We got through the front door just in time.

After that, it was all perfect. Being late October, the weather in Mexico was not too hot, but the ocean still comfortably warm to swim in. We stayed in hostels or cheap hotels. The creaking and grunting coming through the walls at one hotel led us to joke that we were in a whorehouse, only to learn in the morning that it really was one.

We visited Morelia during the Day of the Dead festival, where the whole city is decorated with orange flowers. The residents have dinner and spend the night in the cemetery with their departed relatives. It was interesting to observe, but we had the feeling that we and the other tourists were intruding on their sacred ground.

After looking around Mexico City, we traveled 25 miles northeast to Teotihuacan, the ancient Mesoamerican city

that was once home to over 100,000 people. We climbed the 248 steps to the top of the Pyramid of the Sun, which is about 220 feet high. After that, we headed 490 miles south to Palenque, where the pyramids and palace complex were also very impressive.

I have to say that I was more awe-struck by Bonampak, another ancient dwelling that was a further 170 miles south, close to the border with Guatemala. We hiked through the jungle to get to it, starting at sunrise, and ran a gauntlet of toucans doing flybys and monkeys pelting us with fruit. There was something about the vegetation flowing effortlessly around the ruins of Bonampak that really fired my imagination.

The last pyramid we climbed was the steep El Castillo in Chichen Itza on the Yucatan Peninsula. We then spent a couple of days on the beach near Tulum living in a cabana, a shelter made of wood slats with a thatched roof. Apparently, we got there just in time. I have some Czech friends who

moved to Tulum not too long after that and they told me that cabanas are as much a thing of the past as the pyramids. In their place are hotels catering to tourists willing to pay more to enjoy the natural beauty and history as we did on a budget.

Our flight to Prague from Mexico City required a connection in New York. For that, we had to buy a transit visa for $30, just to set foot on American soil for a few hours. It was December 2001 and the world was still reeling from the shock of 9/11. I was in the employee dining room for an early breakfast when I heard that one of the towers of the World Trade Center was on fire after being hit by a plane.

As it seemed like an accident, I thought of that movie from the seventies, *The Towering Inferno*. It was from listening to people on the slope that I learned that it was a terrorist attack. I could sense a great deal of fear in their expressions. If terrorists could pull off something of this scale right under the FBI's nose, who knew what might come next.

You could see and hear the paranoia everywhere at JFK airport. I got a taste of it when they found a machete in my check-in luggage. It should have been no big deal. The luggage was going in the cargo bay, meaning I would not have access to the machete during the flight, but these were not normal times. I told all the cops and security that showed up that I bought it in Mexico for my trek through the jungle and now I was taking it home as a souvenir. They searched my luggage four times before deciding that I wasn't a threat.

4

WE ARRIVED ON the 1st of December, giving me just a couple of weeks with family and friends before heading back to Sun Valley. For my flight on Christmas Eve, I went to Prague to meet up with a fellow Czech worker who was also going back. When we went to check in at the airport, the clerk told us we were quite early. We told her we just wanted to make sure we didn't miss our flight. No, she told us. We were really early, as in a month too early. Our flight was for January 24th, not December 24th. We checked our tickets and, sure enough, the travel agent in Prague somehow got the months mixed up, and in all that time we didn't notice it.

We were still able to make the first leg of our flight to Frankfurt, but the clerk told us that it was up to Lufthansa Airlines to see if they could do the same for our flight to the U.S. We were nervous as hell for the one hour it took us to reach Frankfurt, but the Lufthansa clerk instantly took our tickets and made it her mission to get them switched. She typed keystroke after keystroke into her computer, all the while we tried not to watch, and after forty minutes, she told us that she found us a flight to New York City, and from there to Salt Lake City. On Christmas Eve. Our savior.

Back again in Sun Valley, I wanted to try a different chair lift and was given the one called Mayday, which went all the way to the top of the mountain. It's one of the oldest lifts still in operation there, just a two-seater, so definitely nothing for Arnold. I worked it with an American named Joe. He was a short, crazy guy who smoked pot and snorted coke in equal amounts.

There were lots of drugs in the dormitory, probably coming from the same source that kept the rich and elite visitors to Sun Valley supplied with whatever substance they were into at the time. Because Joe looked and acted like a stoner, our supervisor kept hinting that he was going to give us a drug test, but it never happened to me in all the seasons I worked there.

My salary was raised to $7.90 an hour, which was still nothing special, so I again looked for an extra job. A restaurant in Ketchum called Chandler's hired me as a busboy to clear the tables, haul the dirty dishes around, keep the salt and pepper shakers full, and whatnot. I got a slice of the tips and a free meal. The tips were great and so was the food, and but the real delight for me was the atmosphere. It was one of those places where you look forward to going to work every day.

I won't deny it. I had a blast in Sun Valley the second time around because I was by myself. With no girlfriend at my side, I was free to hang out wherever and with whomever I wanted. In addition to Joe, I spent a lot of time with any number of the cute girls from Brazil, Columbia, and Poland who worked in Sun Valley.

Already during the first season, the girls from Poland were a source of tension between Lenka and me. She would turn a corner and there I was with a Polish girl, the two of us laughing it up and poking at each other. Our gang regularly met up at Lefty's Bar and Grill. The dogs there were great: a corndog cost $1.25, a hot dog $4.50, a chili dog $6.50. They also had twelve brews on tap, including beer from abroad, but on Sundays, we went to Whiskey Jack's, because all the drinks there were for a dollar.

I brought my snowboard with me, but quickly realized I needed something better, and not least because it was bright red and had a big banana painted on it. I bought a good one from the K2 brand, along with Burton boots and binders, all real quality stuff. I also got a new jacket, gloves, and pads. With a solid decade of snowboarding behind me, I zoomed down Bald Mountain, doing jumps and twists with ease on the fresh, powdery snow. And that's when it hit me. What am I doing operating a lift when I could be teaching snowboarding here?

The company told me they would be happy to hire me as a snowboard instructor once I was certified, but they didn't do that in Sun Valley. I applied to other resorts where it was done and I was accepted at Lake Tahoe on the California-Nevada border. I arranged to spend the next winter season there, working as a lift operator while I took the course necessary for certification. Then I would go back to Sun Valley for the winter season after that.

When I got back to the Czech Republic, I made plans to visit Lenka in Northern Ireland, where she was working as an au-pair. She told me to fly in to Belfast, go to this guy on such-and-such street, and there I could borrow a car. She warned me, however, that English could be a problem.

I told her she was crazy. I work in America. I don't have any problem with English. Of course, she was speaking from experience, and I had no clue what this guy was talking about when we met. We somehow managed to work it out, and I drove away in a Nissan Micra, probably the smallest car in the world at the time. It proved to be a good choice, because many of the country roads in Northern Ireland are extremely narrow.

The natural scenery that awaited us was both beautiful and dramatic, especially the Giant's Causeway on the coast. It consists of 40,000 basalt columns formed by volcanic action millions of years ago, now rising skyward like giant stepping stones. Everywhere we went the people were really friendly, but there was one occasion where we got to see with our own eyes the divisions of the north. We were in a pub in Belfast and everybody was having a good time when a guy who wasn't supposed to be there walked in. A group of pub-goers jumped him, dragged him outside, and left him in a pool of his own blood.

It was, in fact, the parade season, when all the orange comes out, and you could feel the nervousness in the air. The lady Lenka worked for was a cop who drove around the city with a German Shepherd. She was tough as nails, a single mother of three whose boyfriend was this really weird Czech guy. I don't know how they met, but they made a strange couple.

Back home, we immediately made plans to take off again. Actually, we had to go somewhere. It went back to the time just before our trip to America in 2001. I needed a job and found one in a computer company. Since I knew I would be leaving in a couple of months, I spent all my time on the Internet when nobody was looking.

The Internet then was as wild as the market economy, with all kinds of contests inviting people to fill in answers to win a prize. I don't know how many of these contests I entered, but I won the top prize of a travel agency, which was worth 25,000 crowns ($600). Like so many other small businesses, travel agencies were going bust, so we decided to put that money to use while it was still there.

It was enough for two expeditions. The first took us to the Dolomite Mountains of northeastern Italy for climbing via ferrata. This means the routes are already laid out with steel ropes and anchors in the rocks. Climbers put on a harness and clip on to the ropes, both to assist with the climb and to keep from falling off.

Toward the end of our stay, I tackled one of the steepest, most difficult climbs, which was hard enough, but the cold weather that day left my toes and fingers feeling numb. I thought of my uncle Arnošt in the Himalayas, but where he made it to the top, I gave up and descended down to our camp. Exhausted, I collapsed into our tent and missed the campfire that night.

For our next expedition, we joined a group going to Crimea for a bike ride around the perimeter of that peninsula. We camped in tents at night, cooked packets of soup, and ate bread, sausages and spam brought from home. The bike-riding off-road was great, but the roads themselves were treacherous. The locals, for whatever reason, were in the habit of discarding glass bottles on the asphalt, so we had to stop several times to repair flat tires.

We saw lots of classical ruins along the way, also minarets that had been built by the Tartars before they were deported by Stalin. We came across lots of sinkholes filled with water similar to the cenotes in Mexico. I jumped into one of them, about thirty feet high and never felt such icy water in my life.

To get to Yalta, we had to climb nearly 4,000 feet, which seemed to go on forever, but then we glided all the way down to the coast. I thought Yalta would be this posh place full of grand hotels, but there were abandoned construction projects everywhere. Huge, empty monoliths of concrete standing there for who knows how long. Even the beach was mostly laid out in concrete.

While in Crimea, some members of our group had stomach problems. I knew the cause. Our bus had this big water tank, and the guy who organized the trip always filled it up at each stop at a gas station. I took a look inside the tank and noticed there was black mold on the walls.

Whether or not he had meant the water only to be used for washing up, some people were drinking it despite the fact that bottled water in Crimea cost next to nothing. For the long trip home, the toilet on our bus was never unoccupied. Lenka and I didn't drink the water, but we caught it too because the bug turned out to be dysentery, which is highly contagious.

I found that out when I went to the hospital. They immediately put me in quarantine and sent an order to my parents, because they had come into contact with me, to come and join me. My mother and father wisely went to a travel agency instead and caught the next last-minute trip to Turkey.

I ended up in the hospital for a week, but because the staff allowed me to keep my backpack with me, I paid some extra money to get my own room. That way, I could smoke a joint every night from the weed I had in my pack. I opened the window and nobody was any the wiser for it.

5

LENKA AND I HAD a few weeks at home before leaving for California just before Christmas. We flew in to San Francisco and hopped aboard a bus for the two-hundred-mile trip to the resort. Unlike in Sun Valley, we had to arrange our own accommodation and were told the cheapest digs close to Lake Tahoe were in Reno, Nevada. The place we found was super cheap, but also a dump with communal bathrooms.

In fact, all of Reno was dumpy compared to Sun Valley, but the casinos were a distinct advantage. When we got paid in Sun Valley, we cashed or deposited our checks at the local bank. In Reno, we cashed them in the casino because we always got something complimentary like free chips for gambling or drinks at the bar.

Living in Reno meant a commute by bus of thirty-five miles to Lake Tahoe along Interstate 80. Where Sun Valley catered to an exclusive clientele, it seemed everyone went to Tahoe. Its popularity as a tourist destination showed in the long lines everywhere. But even as a lift operator, it never hit me just how long the lines were until we spent a day off at the legendary resort of Squaw Valley on the western shore of the lake.

We had just got on the bus going there when I realized that I had forgotten my jacket. It was sunny outside, but also 5°F (-15°C), not ideal for winter sports in a sweater. I could've gotten off the bus, but I was worried that I would never get another chance to go to Squaw Valley. So I went there and froze my ass off. The wait for the lift was brutal enough, but that long, slow ride to the top was absolute murder.

It was not just because of the crowds that the lifts at Tahoe were a lot harder to work. It snowed there quite a lot and we had to have a broom always handy to sweep the chairs. Another difference with Sun Valley is that we were rotated around the different lifts. There was no getting too comfortable at one location, but the good thing about that was, we got to know a lot more people.

After a month, Lenka and I left the dump in Reno to live in a house next to the lake with six other lift operators. They were two Aussies from Perth named Matt and Matt, a Brazilian couple, and two Argentineans. On nights and weekends, we smoked a lot of grass, drank a lot of whisky, and played a lot of poker, but I can't remember if any of the three had something to do with the Mohawk hairstyle I wore at the time.

But I was mindful of the reason I was there and enrolled myself in a snowboard instructor course. The resort paid for it. All I had to do was pay for the exam, which costs an eye-watering $200. The theory portion was held in a classroom once a week. The point of being an instructor was to be able to explain snowboard moves, not just show them. How to make a hillside turn, how to stop, which methodology to apply for someone who never stepped on a snowboard before. Not as easy as it sounds.

For the practical part, we went to the snow park. That was the one thing missing at Sun Valley, a snowboard park. Usually, I wore only a sweater because it was mostly warm at Lake Tahoe. Really cold days like the one that greeted me at Squaw Valley were quite rare.

At the park, I was in my element. My instructor was surprised at how well I knew how to ride the rails, the big tabletop, and both half pipe and super pipe. I showed him how to master certain maneuvers he didn't know, and he in turn showed me how to do the practical part of the exam perfectly.

The exam was held at the Heavenly resort on the south shore of the lake. My exam instructor was a cool guy, but he wanted to know everything. I did all right on the theory part, but blew him away on the board, including mastering both types of stance.

Snowboarders who ride with the left foot on the nose are regular, those with the right foot are goofy. I'm regular, but learned to ride goofy because that's what my brother is and I was in the habit of borrowing his board. While the other guys in my class struggled with the switch, I breezed through it. The instructor rated me "awesome" and awarded me the bronze certificate and badge, which was the starting level for new instructors.

It was settled. Next season, I was going back to Sun Valley as a snowboard instructor. But it had come at a cost, because paying for the exam, rent, and enjoying Lake Tahoe instead of working all the time left me with little money after the season ended. We decided to stay on in America under a tourist visa and work there illegally. It was a big risk given that if we were caught, I could kiss my Sun Valley dream goodbye.

The deciding factor turned out to be San Francisco. That city held a special allure because of its connection to skateboarding and icons like the Golden Gate Bridge. Our plan was to live and work there until the start of the next season in Sun Valley.

We arrived in April and checked into another dump with a communal bathroom. Being on a busy corner near the financial district, it was noisy and smelled of car exhaust. It was meant to be temporary, but all the rooms or apartments we found in our price range required a three-month deposit. So we lived in squalor, as a friend called it, for the five months that we were there.

But it didn't matter, because we were in San Francisco. We toured Alcatraz, visited the City Lights Bookstore and other hangouts of the Beat Generation, and even located the original Levi's store. We were proud to call their famous jeans by their actual name and not *levvies* as they are known back home.

For work, Lenka got a job at Starbucks and I sold Hawaiian shirts at a store on the Fisherman's Wharf. The owners were a very nice couple who knew my work status, but didn't care so long as I had a social security number. I also worked as a cashier for a gas station three nights a week in the area known as Japantown. The owner was a Russian guy who also didn't care about my expired work visa.

At a certain time at night, I locked the front door and handled all transactions through a window tray. One night, I was just minutes away from locking the front door when a Japanese guy came in and wanted to prepay for his gas using a $100 bill. Having never seen a $100 bill before, I was suspicious and held it under a special light we had to detect counterfeit bills. The light showed none of the fibers inside real bills, so I pushed it back to him and told him to get lost. When I told the Russian about it, he told me to take any counterfeit hundreds in the future because he collects them. I thought that was weird, but he offered me fifty bucks for each.

The next week, another Japanese guy came in and tried to pass me a counterfeit $100 bill. I told him to beat it but kept the bill. He grumbled and left and I thought no more of it. A few hours later, I was already locked up when another Japanese guy came up to the door to tell me that there was some guy lying on the bathroom floor unconscious. I got up, unlocked the door, stepped outside, and locked the door behind me.

At that moment, six Japanese guys came running at me out of hiding. I immediately knew that I had been set up and took off. One of them shot me with a Taser, which I felt in my back but it failed to stun me. I made it across the street to another gas station, but the guy behind the cashier window was asleep. By then, the gang was on top of me and beat me unconscious with wooden clubs.

When I came to, the cashier and a plainclothes cop were standing next to me. There was blood all over me because the clubs had been dipped in glue, then rolled in tiny fragments of glass. I told the cop what had happened and made the mistake of showing him the counterfeit bill, because he took it and never gave it back to me. Before leaving the scene, he told me that they would check all the footage from the CCTV cameras and let me know once they apprehended the gang. I never heard from him again.

But he did do me a big favor by driving me to the hospital. At first, he wanted to call an ambulance, but I knew that you paid for such service in America. The Russian guy felt bad about getting me into this mess and paid all my hospital bills. They included another trip back there when the cuts around my left elbow became re-infected. The doctor cleaned them up, but told me that some of the glass was probably still in there.

We made two big trips while living in San Francisco. For the first one, we headed south to Sequoia National Park. No words can describe the moment you stand next to those majestic trees. Touching a living thing more than three thousand years old feels like reaching back into time. From there, we touched the outskirts of Death Valley before turning north for Mono Lake, which is a salt lake in the middle of the desert. We continued north to Lake Tahoe because we wanted to see what it looked like in summer time. In winter, when we were there, the water is generally choppy. We could never imagine such a beautiful sight as the dazzling blue color of the lake that greeted our return.

Our second big trip took us down the coast to visit Matt and Matt in San Diego. We left late at night, so that by morning, I told Lenka I was too tired to drive anymore. We were outside Los Angeles and she was afraid of driving through the city. So I pulled into a gas station, got some coffee, threw water on my face in the men's room, and hit the road again.

It couldn't have been more than five minutes later when the car started shaking as it drifted onto the shoulder. I woke up and instinctively hit the brakes, which caused the car to spin out of control and bounce off the guard railing several times before coming to a rest. It was still before sunrise on a Saturday morning, so fortunately there were no cars in front or in back of us.

The car ran fine all the way to San Diego, but when we got out of it, we could see that it was basically totaled. All four doors, both bumpers, front grill, the entire body was covered in dents and scratches. We took out full insurance coverage, so it didn't wreck our weekend with Matt and Matt or our look around San Diego.

The next day I called the rent-a-car company to report the accident. They were pretty cool about it, but advised me

to inform the police. I couldn't do that because we had spent the night before with Matt and Matt partying and getting high. One look at me and the cops would draw their own conclusions on the cause of the accident.

After getting back to San Francisco, we were broke and exhausted. Since it was only August, we decided to go home and rest before the start of the 2003-04 season in Sun Valley. It wasn't hard to say goodbye to San Francisco. It's a beautiful city full of friendly, helpful people, but we struggled to live there. Everything is unbelievably expensive and the glamour quickly fades every time you meet another homeless person or drug addict on the street.

6

IN THE THREE MONTHS before we left for the States again, I worked for a friend of mine named Igor. He owned a company that installed epoxy floors for factories, stadiums, and other large-scale projects. He was planning to take a crew to Holland for several weeks and I jumped at the chance to join them.

It was about wanderlust and adventure, not money. The one rule I gave myself for working in America was to save at least $2,000 every month, and I now had three seasons, or twelve months, behind me. In that time, I had gone from being indebted up to my neck to relative prosperity.

My job was to mix the epoxy, put it in a wheel barrel, and bring it to the guys laying the floor, who poured, leveled and smoothed it. It was real unskilled stuff, but the physical nature of it was a relief from what I had been doing for the past two years. We got $60 a day, which was about the same as in Sun Valley, but also breakfast and dinner, a boxed lunch, and an open bar at the hotel as far as beer was concerned. Taken together with the camaraderie of the crew and all the weed that was available in Holland, it turned out to be quite a nice working vacation.

Although Lenka had sworn off Sun Valley after that first season there, she came back with me in December 2003 to see more of America. First, we got off the plane in New York and spent a week there before heading west. We toured the galleries, saw the Flatiron Building, Washington Square and

Brooklyn Bridge. Recovery was still going on at Ground Zero, which was enclosed with green tarp to keep tourists from getting too close. We went to the top of the Empire State Building and from there we could see how empty the skyline of Manhattan now seemed to be.

Returning to Sun Valley after two years, I found the gang still there with the exception of Joe. He had moved on to the Big Sky resort in Montana, probably to stay ahead of the stoner police. Of course, I couldn't just pick up where I left off the last time. I had Lenka with me, and, as a bronze certificate holder, I would be training only children that season. I wouldn't be able to get away with showing up hung-over and glassy-eyed the way I often did at the lift station.

Snowboarding school was completely flexible. It could be just a morning or afternoon, a single day or more. For some kids, it was like a winter camp. Their parents dropped them off and picked them up after a week, but they didn't go home in the meantime. The parents went to the mountain next door to ski for that week. They had a good time, their kids had a good time, but none of it was spent together.

My workday began when I arrived at the lodge with the other instructors. Our uniform consisted of a standard-issue red jacket and black pants that made us clearly identifiable on the slopes. The supervisor classified the students according to their experience and ability and allotted them to the instructors.

Morning sessions ran from nine to twelve with anywhere from six to twelve children. After leaving the lift, I led them to our spot, did a bit of stretching exercise with them, and then showed them what it was all about. Basically, it was learning how to ride on the edge of their board using their toes or heels for balance.

I tried to make it fun by goofing off with them during breaks and lunch time. For those who were shy or scared, I ran alongside the board holding their hands. It paid off when the parents opted for private lessons and the kids chose me. I normally got $13 an hour, but for a weeklong private lesson, the parents might tip me $100, $150, even $200.

A private lesson could also be like babysitting. Once I was handed a four-year-old boy despite the prohibition against teaching snowboarding to kids under the age of six (because it can really mess up their spine). The boy already knew how to snowboard, so it was just the two of us doing the slope while his parents were busy elsewhere that day.

For one extended break, Lenka and I rented a car and we drove three hundred miles northwest to the Big Sky resort in Montana. It was great hanging out with Joe again and the resort certainly lived up to its name. It had so much open space compared to Lake Tahoe, which felt cramped because of all the trees. We took the lift up, walked past a sign warning us to have our avalanche equipment ready, and sailed down the wide slopes.

From Big Sky, we went south to a ski resort near Jackson Hole, Wyoming. I would rate it the best of all the resorts we visited. It had a lot of powdery snow, lots of open space, and a magnificent view of the Grand Teton Mountains. It felt like there were no slopes at all there. You could take your board practically anywhere and have a great time.

It was a fantastic trip, but back in Sun Valley, the tension between Lenka and me was no longer deniable. Here I was teaching the children of the rich and famous while she, the former au-pair, was stuck doing unskilled work. She found the resort no better in winter than in summer, and like our first season there together, she hardly ever saw me.

Besides teaching snowboarding and waiting tables at Chandler's restaurant, I spent weekends away at a resort close to Boise to earn my silver certification for snowboard instructors. But one time she saw me all too clearly, on our last night there no less, in the romantic embrace of a Slovak girl, and that finished it between us.

We had been together for nine years and lately it felt like an open relationship. She later told me that she had carried on with someone while we were together at Lake Tahoe. We nevertheless went ahead with our plan to see the American southwest before going home. We left Sun Valley in April for a drive of 850 miles to Keystone, Colorado, where my friend Michal Štefek, the one who convinced me to go to America, worked in a ski rental shop.

Mindful of how I fell asleep on the road while driving down the California coast, I asked Joe if he had something to help me stay awake for the long drive. I already tried several stimulants in pill form, but nothing worked. He told me to go to a gas station along the interstate and buy Yellow Jacket. They were pills that contained a really strong herbal stimulant. I got me a box of three for $20, took one pill, and drove the entire eighteen hours to Keystone wide-eyed.

The season was already over in Sun Valley, but they still had plenty of powdery snow in the Rocky Mountains. It was spring but felt like winter there. Michal took us to Arapahoe Basin and again we were in awe of the tremendous amount of open space in these resorts. Czech slopes by comparison are not for the claustrophobic. It was a nice, refreshing break, which we needed for the trip ahead.

We went south to Four Corners, to stand where Arizona, Colorado, New Mexico, and Utah meet, and also to see the Pueblo cliff dwellings. Then it was west to Monument Valley, which all Europeans know of from the westerns, Grand Canyon, Hoover Dam and lastly Las Vegas. We took lots of pictures, not just of the natural beauty of America, but of what we Europeans think of as Americana, like the small store in the middle of nowhere with a big "Liquor" sign, a phone booth and ice box outside.

In all, we covered a thousand miles from Colorado to Nevada, most of it doable with another Yellow Jacket pill. All that was left was to drive from Vegas to Sun Valley to pick up our luggage, another 580 miles. I popped the remaining pill and drove thirty-six hours virtually nonstop. It would no longer be possible the following year, because they completely banned Yellow Jacket in America.

7

THE HECTIC DRIVE through the southwest United States reignited the relationship between Lenka and me. When we got back, we decided to give it another try and went to England together to visit another former classmate. After hanging out with her in London, we took a bus north to Scotland. We climbed Ben Nevis, the highest peak in Britain, and saw the famous Loch Ness. To see more of the spectacular landscape, we set out to hitchhike to Inverness, the largest city of the Highlands.

Nobody would pick us up. We stood there for four or five hours in the wind and rain and nothing. In all our years of hitchhiking, we had always found a ride. This was our first failure and it was depressing. Even when we had troubles on the road, whether with wild dogs stalking us in Greece or dealing with the flat tire in Sweden, we always managed to stay above the gloom. But as car after car passed us by, all we could do was gripe and complain. It seemed an indication that we were fooling ourselves. Our relationship was over. After visiting Glasgow and Edinburgh, we headed home and went our separate ways.

I returned to England for a couple of weeks in October with Igor and crew to lay a floor for a new music hall in Newcastle. It was more of me transporting barrels of polyurethane, mixing up the compound and bringing it to the guys to pour and smooth. I certainly didn't need the money. What I made from tips alone in Sun Valley put me in the same earnings bracket as a top manager in the Czech Republic, but the pull of travel and camaraderie was irresistible as ever.

My parents were quite proud of how far I had come. True, I was twenty-seven and rootless, but I indulged my wanderlust while at the same time made excellent money. I didn't spend the offseason sitting on their couch drinking beer and smoking pot, rather I worked for a solid Czech company. I drank beer and smoked pot, but only with my friends, and only on one occasion did it get me into hot water with my mother.

It was my sister's fortieth birthday party and we were all celebrating in a restaurant with karaoke, dancing, lots of games and goofing off. A couple of us convinced my dad, who's a smoker, to try some pot. So he did, and did he ever float through the room for the rest of the evening. My mother was furious. She thought it was a disgraceful way to act, both him and us. She really let me have it, but it went deeper than the weed.

I had the feeling she was worried I might never come back from America, that I would eventually settle down there. We never really talked about it, but the closest I came to staying there happened after I arrived for the 2004-05 season. With my silver certification, I could teach adults, and two young women signed up for a one-day course just before New Year's. I hit it off with one of them, Jessica, who was spending the holidays in Sun Valley with a rich uncle. I got her number, and the next month I flew to her home in Seattle to spend the weekend.

That happened two more times. I really liked her, I liked Seattle and that whole area. We went to the Olympic Mountains and rented mountain bikes there. I could imagine settling down there with her. And then in March, she told me she was going back to her ex-boyfriend. It was over, just like that. Later, I suspected she had been hoping for that all along. I was just a fling to help make it happen. Whatever the case, I limped back to Sun Valley and focused on getting my gold certification.

I certainly wasn't miserable that season. A group of snowboard instructors from Australia were there, and one of them, Mark Wojtas, became my roommate. As his last name suggests, he had a Polish grandfather who came from a place very close to the Czech border. I told the Australians that after I got my certification at Lake Tahoe, I applied to several resorts in Australia to teach snowboarding there. None of them replied. They told me that there were only a few foreign instructors there and most of them came from Austria. Seeing my work firsthand in Sun Valley, these guys put in a good word for me with their resort and I got a visa to work there during the upcoming summer.

One weekend, we all took off for Canyons Resort in Utah. They wanted to introduce me to their coach, Grant, who would also train me. A bit older than the rest of us, Grant was a real likeable guy whose skill and precision were nothing like I had ever seen before. He was a snowboarder's snowboarder. He led us to the Snowbird resort, just east of Salt Lake City. It's a huge place, with lots of steep sections. It was there that I got to experience my first real free ride.

We took the lift to the top, then carried our boards about a mile to this point which, in my mind, might as well have been a cliff. He told me and the others not to freak out, just to get on our boards and do exactly what he says. We should start off by making four small turns, the smallest we can manage, and after that let loose. Once we reached the forest, we should stop and wait for him to lead us through there, because it was full of rocks.

I could see what he was doing. Grant wanted to know if I had it in me to be an instructor under his guidance. I was scared shitless, but I went over the edge and did exactly what he told me. Not only did everything work out perfectly, but the rush of adrenaline was nothing like I had ever felt before, not even bungee jumping. I sailed all the way to the forest and stopped. Grant came up to me, pulled up his goggles and said, "Good. You can go to Australia."

As the season came to an end, Mark and I decided to go to British Columbia to do some heli-snowboarding, where a helicopter would take us up to the top of a mountain and we would sail down it off-trail. In order to qualify, we had to undergo an avalanche survival course and buy complete avalanche gear. But they ended up canceling it because there was hardly any snow in the mountains. British Columbia had its worst snowfall in twenty years. They refunded our deposit, but we got stuck with the expensive avalanche gear. It's still in my garage today.

When I told two Czech girls working as lift operators that British Columbia was off, they begged me to go with them to Hawaii after the season ended. Thinking it might be my only chance to see Hawaii, I went with them. Before we left, I went to the library to learn everything I could about Maui, but when I told the girls about all the things we could see and do there, they weren't interested. They only wanted to spend all day at the beach or by the pool.

I ended up doing most of the sightseeing on my own, but Maui was worth it. I got to explore bamboo forests, poked my way around beaches shaped by lava rock, and snorkeled alongside clownfish and sea turtles. A real treat was the fabulous banyan tree in Lahaina. It's so expansive from its base trunk that the canopy actually covers two-thirds of an acre.

I managed to get the girls to come with me to see some waterfalls and I joined them on a whale-watching excursion. The guide told us there was no guarantee we would see anything and for the longest time we didn't. Then suddenly a huge humpback whale rose up not even ten yards from our boat. Everyone on deck got drenched when it flopped back into the sea. The excursion was shaping up to be nothing more than that one hit and run, but a pod of whales soon appeared and we forgot all about our wet clothes.

A trip to Haleakala Crater was a must, but the girls shook their heads when I told them we had to get up at three in the morning. I read that it could be quite cold there in the predawn hours, so I took my winter jacket from Sun Valley with me just in case. It was a smart move, because it was

absolutely freezing when I took a picture of the breathtaking sunrise.

But then, an hour after I entered the crater, I was wearing only a shirt and shorts. Another hour after that, it was only the shorts, but it never got as hot as the active volcano of Popocatépetl near Mexico City. The landscape of Haleakala resembled the moon or some extraterrestrial world. I walked inside the crater for five hours before I came out on the other side and hitched a ride back to my car.

Since it was Hawaii, I had to give surfing a go. The guy who rented me the board pointed out places on the map where I could go, adding that the best spot was off-limits because sharks were known to appear there. If I decided I wanted to try it anyway, he advised me to do it only if there were locals there.

There were some guys there, so I had at it. At some point, I noticed all of them paddling in, but it didn't register with me until they all started screaming at me and pointing. I looked behind me and, sure enough, there was a dorsal fin. I freaked out a little but managed to paddle in to safety. It was when I stood up on the beach with my board in hand that I noticed all the blood everywhere.

Unlike the other surfers, I had gone out there bare-chested and rubbed my nipples raw on the rough surface of the board when I was paddling. That shark may have had a bead on me and now other sharks were cruising offshore as well. I quickly left before the locals chased me off.

That little mishap aside, Hawaii had been a dream. In the end, I was happy to have my avalanche gear and nothing to show for it. I was, however, eager to get back to the Czech

Republic. Not because I had only a month before I had to catch a flight to Australia, but because there was somebody back home I wanted to see.

Before leaving for Sun Valley, I got to know this girl I met a few years earlier through the same group of people we hang out with. Like me, Kamča (from Kamila) loves to travel and see new places. After graduating from design school, she went to Munich to au-pair for a lovely couple with three kids. When she came back, she enrolled in a school to learn ergotherapy, which helps people with physical or mental disabilities achieve a greater quality of life.

She had a boyfriend at the time, but it was so much fun talking to her that we exchanged emails before I left. We wrote regularly, and she was the one I poured my heart out to after Jessica cheated on me. She wrote back amazed. Her boyfriend had cheated on her too! That set off a flurry of letters that led us to falling in love when I got back in late April.

We spent some time in Prague, where we met up with Mirek, my skateboarding mentor, and his girlfriend. We had a romantic evening together before she took me to the station for my bus to Vienna. It was just like in the movies. An emotional farewell, the bus leaving, and Kamča waiting and waving until it was well out of sight.

Sad as I was to leave her at that moment, Qatar Airlines did their best to cheer me up. The seats in the tourist class were nice and roomy and above you the ceiling lit up like the night sky. On crappier airlines, you're crammed into a seat with a small screen in front of you. The food on Qatar was gourmet, and when I asked for a beer and whiskey, the flight attendant handed me both and told me to hop on back any time for a refill.

I had a stopover in Dubai, so I arranged my flight out of there for four days later. The old part of the city was very nice, whereas the new part was the biggest construction site I have ever seen. The sail-shaped hotel Burj Al Arab was standing, but most of what makes Dubai iconic today was still under construction. That included the Palm Islands and Burj Khalifa, now the tallest building in the world.

What's interesting is, they had only dug the hole for the Burj Khalifa, but I saw several postcards showing it already built and standing in Dubai. In fact, I couldn't find a single postcard of Dubai without the future skyscraper in the picture.

8

MARK WAS WAITING for me when I arrived in Melbourne in late June. We got into the car and headed 220 miles northeast for Dinner Plain, which is a small bedroom community close to Mount Hotham resort. There I lived in a townhouse with several other employees. Because there was only one small expensive store in Dinner Plain, two of us made a ninety-minute run to the city of Albury every couple of weeks for food and supplies. I always volunteered to go and convinced whoever went with me to do some sight-seeing along the way.

Snowboard school started at eight-thirty, half an hour earlier than at Sun Valley. On Tuesdays, we had to come in an hour before that for our weekly training with Grant. One of the tricks he used to refine our skills was to blindfold us. He didn't mean it as a "feel the force" kind of thing, rather he wanted us to learn to trust our feet to do the guiding. Another was to draw us the line of direction on a map or picture. Once we got to the terrain, we took turns leading on that line, but it wasn't easy matching what we had seen on the map with what we now saw in front of us.

The differences between Mount Hotham and Sun Valley were many. For starters, there was the snow. Aussie-grade powder was nowhere near the quality of powder in America. You could feel what a slog it was to slice through the snow down under. Then there was the pay, which was variable. Employees at Mount Hotham started at the lowest hourly rate and were given raises for every fifty hours or so that they worked. The idea was to keep them from taking off in the middle of the season. By the time the season ended, I was making almost double the wages I started out with.

There were also no tips, which was probably because the courses were expensive to begin with. In fact, winter sports in Australia have gone up so drastically that Mark recently informed me that he goes abroad for snowboarding. And because the courses are so expensive, the clients always show up. In America, no-shows are common if it's snowing heavily or windy and cold outside or the client just doesn't feel like it.

In Australia, they never missed a lesson. The weather was pretty crappy during the 2005 season, the worst in twenty years, I was told. It rained for at least a third of it, but no matter what, they were always there, studiously learning their turns even in the rain.

I had a great desire to see New Zealand when the season came to an end in September, but did the math and figured that one week there would cost me the same as three weeks in Australia. So I went to Melbourne with Mark and met his large family. I toured the museum where Ned Kelly was imprisoned and executed. A bunch of Mark's cousins, including a huge guy called Lumberjack, took me to the forest outside the city to shoot guns and camp overnight.

We then headed up to the coast towards Adelaide to do some surfing, but like in Hawaii, I had no easy time of it. These guys were great surfers and used short boards to rip through the waves. No one had a long board for me to use like the one I had in Hawaii. Getting up and standing on a short board proved to be a huge challenge for me. Even paddling on it was a lot harder. By the time we left the beach, I was totally exhausted and had only one small wave to show for it.

There was no missing a chance to see Sydney, but I found the vibe there much edgier than in Melbourne. At the famous Bondi Beach, I saw a couple of surfers in the water actually brawling over the waves. I met up with some friends I worked with at Mount Hotham and together we visited the wilderness outside Sydney. One of them lived with his parents in a very remote area. They too had a large collection of guns, but what I really liked was his compound bow. It had cables and pulleys strung together from one end of the bow to the other. It took almost no effort to let the arrows fly from it.

I later bought a similar bow in America and took it back with me to the Czech Republic. As things had calmed down a bit since 9/11, no one gave me any grief over the bow and arrows packed away in my luggage. Apparently, the incident with "Machete Mike" at Kennedy Airport a few years earlier had been long forgotten.

I then reconnected with my friends in Melbourne and we set out on the Great Ocean Road. The coastline was absolutely stunning, particularly the point known as the Twelve Apostles. These are limestone stacks that rise a hundred and fifty feet or so from the surf. During July, while I was working at Mount Hotham, one of the stacks collapsed, leaving eight standing when I reached the viewpoint in October.

I flew out to Perth for a couple of days to visit Matt and Matt, my friends and roommates from Lake Tahoe. They had to work on one of the days, so I took a ferry out to Rottnest Island, rented a mountain bike and went from beach to beach, encountering no one. Despite the arrival of spring in Australia, I was all alone on this enchanted paradise in the Indian Ocean, sitting on the whitest sand imaginable and looking out over the turquoise water.

Since my flight home left from Melbourne, I went back there and met up with the gang one more time. At the airport, we had a couple of beers in the car and Lumberjack pulled out a bong from under his seat. I was completely zonked by the time I boarded the plane but somehow I made it to my seat.

As before, I was offered a layover in Dubai, but I passed on it. That's a decision I regret, because they opened a snowboarding hall in the six months since I was there. I knew about it but thought it was no big deal at the time. Now I wished I had tried snowboarding in the desert just for the pleasure of saying I did it.

When I was accepted as an instructor at Mount Hotham, my plan was to spend summers working there and winters in Sun Valley, but meeting Kamila changed everything. Australia had been a truly amazing experience and I met a lot of wonderful people there, some of whom became friends for life, but I was twenty-eight-years old and ready to settle down with her. It was time to move on, and so, as I arrived in Sun Valley for the 2005-06 winter season, I knew it was for the last time.

Now a gold-certified veteran, I was at the top of my game. I became a supervisor and enjoyed the power and status that went with the position. That was another big difference between Sun Valley and Mount Hotham. The Aussies are big on fair play. They rank their snowboard instructors according to several factors like certification, seniority and, naturally, what the clients think of you. That ranking then determines the amount of work you get, which clients you get, and so forth.

In Sun Valley, the supervisors alone decided the assignment of work and they played favorites. An instructor who rubbed them the wrong way could expect to go home if there weren't enough students that day. I admit I did the same thing. I came to the lodge, classified the students, and assigned them according to the instructors I liked and those I liked a lot less.

For example, there was this one dumb fuck who always had the raccoon face. That's when you spend all day on the slopes but forget to put sunscreen on the exposed part of your face. Never mind the responsibility factor, this guy looked too scary to tell a child, "That man over there will be your teacher today."

I also got to pick and choose my own clientele. I enjoyed teaching kids, but they learn really quick. One day they're squatting on their boards, creeping along, the next day they're flying down the slope. With adults, the lessons can go on indefinitely.

There were exceptions, though, like this fifty-year-old woman who came to me as a complete beginner. She not only mastered the basics in one morning session, but she actually started to carve in her turns. Where typical beginners turn on the board by skidding with the nose and tail in opposite directions, she cut through the snow with the edge of her board like a knife through butter. For our afternoon session, I had to lead her next door to Bald Mountain just to keep up the challenge for her.

I also continued to work at Chandler's as I had for all my previous seasons. Each year I went up a notch in position. My second season I served the meals, the third season I was a waiter, my fourth I recommended the wine. A lot of our wine came from Napa Valley and I regret never making an excursion there when I lived in San Francisco. Some firsthand knowledge of the vineyards would have made a nice touch.

The clientele I had no problem selling wine to were groups of mature women, which is to say between thirty and fifty thereabouts. Picking up on my accent, they decided I was the tall, dark and mysterious stranger from beyond the seas they had been dreaming about all their lives. They had an endless good time with me, laughing and giggling and not shy at all about grabbing me or nudging me with their thighs and feet. At first, it was cute, but it got old and annoying really quick. Groups of mature men could also be loud and obnoxious, but they never bothered me.

Two good friends and co-workers at Chandler's opened their house up to me and Kamča when she came to visit me for a couple of weeks. She loved it in Sun Valley. It was a great season, with lots of powder and the opening of the first snow park in Sun Valley. I knew all the supervisors and mechanics who worked on the lifts and we regularly hopped rides with them on their snowmobiles.

I introduced her to the Czech people who were working there and Kamča hung out with them while I was working. One night, while I was still at Chandler's, she partied late with them at the dormitory. I told her not to miss the last bus to Elkhorn, where we were staying, else she would have a fourteen-mile hike in the snow in front of her.

She got on the bus all right, but missed her stop in Elkhorn and ended up on the far side of the village. Not knowing where she was, she began knocking on doors and asking the occupants for help. None of them knew the people she mentioned, but one guy kindly gave her a lift in his pickup truck to the stop where she was supposed to get off and from there she found her way back safely.

Kamča left with great memories, but the trip home for her was an ordeal because of me. Since I already had so much stuff to take back with me, I asked her to take my mountain bike with her. The box weighed fifty pounds and she had to haul it around JFK airport along with her luggage.

After landing in Prague, she had to make her way to the bus station with it. The driver took one look at the box and shook his head. In the end, she had to slip him some money to be cool about it. She later told me that she suspected I had concocted the whole thing as a test of love. I swear I didn't. I'm just a guy who doesn't think sometimes.

9

FOR OUR FIRST FEW months back in the Czech Republic we stayed with Kamča's mother Alča. She's a remarkable lady, full of energy and kindness, perfect for her current job as a care provider. Before that, she worked as a seamstress while raising four children. Kamča is the middle of her three daughters.

With the money I saved up in America, we bought a two-bedroom apartment close to the city center. Being on the first floor, it had no view or balcony, but I have great memories of this place. It was our first home together, we had lots of parties with our friends, and our first two children were born while we were living there.

Kamča had finished her studies and was working as an ergo therapist at a health clinic. I got a job that went back to my university days. My boyhood friend and fellow student Michal Milota sometimes worked for Mattes, a wholesale distributor that sent an army of sales reps to small stores with the various commodities they imported from abroad.

Mattes was started by Michal's brother Čeněk and Čeněk's friend and former high school classmate Tomáš. If one of those sales reps turned up sick or AWOL or got fired, they asked him to go in his place. Sometimes they needed two reps and Michal recommended me. So, in addition to being a stockbroker while in school, I also sold toothpaste made in India and toothbrushes in China.

By 2006, the big retail chains were everywhere, and

Mattes was supplying them with their goods. Tomáš, now the sole owner, divided the country into ten regions, each under a different sales manager. When he heard I was back for good, he invited me in for an interview. To show me how much he really wanted me for his team, he said he would fire one of his regional managers and give me his job. I later found out that he was going to fire the man anyway, but that's what made Tomáš such a successful salesman in the first place. He knows how to sell.

I got the guy's region and his company car, one of the smallest you can imagine, and off I went. I liked the work because I always liked selling things. The downside was dealing with the retail chains. You walk in, they hand you a list of what they want, in what volume and at what price, and that's it. No selling, no discussion, take it or leave it.

But I was happy to get out of the office. Mattes was located in a building with shitty windows and no insulation. The place was cold as hell in winter. My salary wasn't great either, less than what I earned in America, but Tomáš promised to make me a senior sales manager within a year and kept his word. I got a much bigger car and had twelve guys working for me covering the entire country.

With my new car and position, Kamča and I decided to get married the next time we went on vacation. Since we had already planned to go to southern Bohemia with Michal Milota and his wife and young son, along with our dog and their dog, I arranged to have our wedding in the town hall of Český Krumlov with the Milotas as our witnesses. A couple of weeks after we got back, we threw a huge reception for our families and friends at a nice lodge in the mountains.

A little over a year later, on September 15, 2008, our first son Olda was born. That was a tough experience. After fifteen hours of labor, Kamča had no more energy to push, so the doctor decided to vacuum the baby out. He created a suction while another doctor dug his forearm into Kamča's upper abdomen and pushed with all his might. I held Kamča's hand and was amazed at how quick it was after that. Kamča was naturally exhausted but fine, the baby was fine, and at thirty-one, I was a dad for the first time.

Olda was an incredible baby. All he did was sleep. He slept all day, all night, we even had to wake him up for his feedings. After we brought him home, we had a party in our apartment for thirty people, with music and games, and he snoozed all through it. When he was awake, he was easy-going about everything. We would stop in a restaurant or pub for lunch and he would sit there all quiet, just taking in the world around him.

Two of the guests at our party as new parents were our neighbors from the fourth floor. They were Marek, another employee of Mattes, and his partner Marcela, who I grew up with, also in the same building. Since Marek and Marcela already had an infant daughter, the four of us bought a baby monitor with the longest range of communication. That way we could get together upstairs or downstairs while the babies slept.

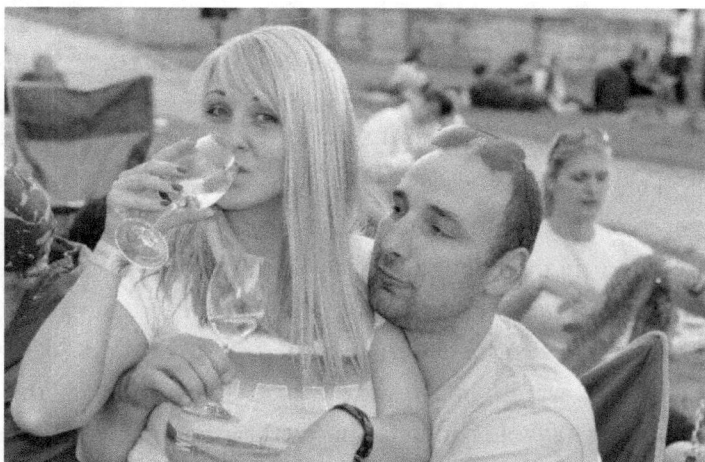

Other times, just the girls went out while the guys helped themselves to wine and cheese or vice versa. Olda being a great sleeper, we usually met upstairs, but there was that time or two when he would stir and then I raced down to our apartment to give him a hug and sing him a lullaby, all the while Marek monitored my progress up above. Once Olda was asleep again, I crept back upstairs for some more wine and cheese.

In 2010, the four of us took our toddlers to Croatia for ten days. We rented a small house that turned out to be so far from the sea that we had to drive to it. The services there were also pretty lousy because it was the end of the season. Despite all that, we had a wonderful time. The weather was good and the water warm. After spending the day by the sea, we came back, put the kids to sleep, then broke out the wine, cheese, and cards for the night.

At this time, I had a new position in the company. Tomáš acquired a new product for his portfolio, a condom made in Thailand that was sold in the Czech and Slovak Republics. He told me it was my baby. I could sell it however I wanted so long as it was the cheapest condom in town. That was his whole sales philosophy. Make something cheap and people will buy it.

That meant keeping costs down, which is why Tomáš never did marketing. His idea of marketing was splashing the logo of the condom across my company car. In one amusing episode, Kamča took this car to the supermarket, where a couple of guys were hanging around outside. Seeing her walk towards the entrance with Olda in her arms, they joked that she sold condoms, but never used them.

It was at this time that I got my first big health scare. Ever since I was attacked by that gang in San Francisco, small bumps sometimes formed around my left elbow. I squeezed them and out came blood and bits of the glass that was still lodged under my skin. Now, a new bump formed, but no matter how hard I squeezed it, nothing came out. I went to a doctor, who arranged to have the glass cut out after they applied a local anesthetic. My appointment was in two weeks.

During those fourteen days, I started having breathing problems. It got so bad that I was unable to climb the eight steps to our apartment. Our family doctor sent me to the pulmonology unit at the hospital, where I was diagnosed with sarcoidosis, an autoimmune disease that causes clusters of inflammation inside the body, particularly in the lungs.

They admitted me immediately, putting me in a room with three other men. Kamča brought me my toothbrush and other personal items. The poor girl was so afraid. I was too after the old man in my room with emphysema, who gasped for air the whole night, died and was wheeled out after I woke up.

I threw all my energy into learning more about sarcoidosis. When I read that it was an overreaction of the immune system, I got an idea that I shared with the head doctor when he stopped by on his rounds. What if my immune system kicked into overdrive because of this emerging piece of glass? At first, he was a dick about it, but he heard me out and arranged to have the remaining pieces of glass in my arm cut out the next morning. Within a couple of days, the worst of my symptoms had disappeared. They kept me for a few more days, then discharged me.

The head doctor warned me to stay away from the sauna, but other than that, I was free to do what I wanted. Let my body be my guide, he told me. Another doctor, who had previously been the head doctor, told me that sometimes people are in the hospital for months before the disease stabilizes. She was totally against discharging me after just ten days. I should take her advice and do nothing except lie on my back.

Even though I was still breathing with difficulty, I

decided to test myself with my snowboard and dog on a hill with no lift. I had to stop to catch my breath every ten steps or so up the slope. Clearly, I wasn't out of the woods yet. I was given corticosteroids to suppress my immune system. The side effects were terrible. Never mind the moon face they give you, the weight gain was ridiculous. I shot up to 250 pounds, which looked bad on my slim frame.

While in the hospital, I began thinking I needed a career change. I had taken the condoms about as far as they could go and working for Tomáš meant endless meetings and phone calls. One evening, he called while Kamča and I were with another couple. My better instincts told me not to answer it, but I did. There was Tomáš, going on and on about stuff we could easily talk about the next day. Finally, I told him we were with some friends, but I would be in his office first thing in the morning.

I no sooner walked through the door of my own office when I was told he wanted to see me immediately. He told me that he was deducting 5,000 crowns, then about $250, from my next payday as a warning to me and everyone else to talk to the boss when he calls. I thought he was joking or just threatening, but he really did it. When I saw that, I said, "Fucking prick. I'm outta here."

I went to Prague for a couple of interviews with multinational companies looking for sales managers. A friend of mine directed me closer to home. It was a gigantic steelworks that under the communist regime employed almost 40,000 people. Long since privatized, its current workforce was barely ten percent of that number. My interview for their sales department went really well. I had literally checked every box on the paper in front of the interviewer. There was just one final question: what kind of salary was I looking for?

I was making 30,000 crowns ($1,500) a month, nothing special for a sales manager but twice the average salary in that region. So I told the guy anything between 35,000 ($1,750) and 45,000 ($2,250) would do. His whole countenance suddenly changed and I knew then and there I didn't get the job. I thought I had overshot the mark he was looking for, but it turns out that I had undervalued myself. If I had asked for 80,000 crowns ($4,000), they would have hired me, maybe not at that salary, but they would have been assured of my confidence and leadership abilities.

It was a good lesson, because right around that time I met up with Igor again. I was telling him he should start his own company in the Czech Republic instead of hiring himself and his crew out to foreign companies, but he felt that poured floors were still too much of a novelty here. Now, in 2010, he told me he was ready to launch such a company and wanted me to be the sales manager. What salary did I want?

Without batting an eye, I told him, "80,000 crowns."

"Done," he said.

The next day, I told Tomáš that I was handing in my notice, which by law was three months. He told me it was too early. I should stay on for at least six months or even a year. That's one thing I learned about every business owner in this country. When they hire you, they want you now, but when you leave them, they try to delay your departure as long as possible.

I told him it was three months and history. He looked at me and said, "You're young and I'm old" (in fact he's only eight years older) "and one thing you'll learn in life is this: As you get older, you lose friends along the way. Today, you just lost one." He then told me to never come back.

We crossed paths professionally in the years afterwards. I only came back to Mattes once more, to a party held on the premises outside. I noticed that the building looked as shitty as ever. I asked Tomáš why, after all these years, with all the millions he has made, why he didn't make the place, if not presentable, at least comfortable to work in. He told me, "Start your own business, then ask me."

Fair enough, but I added that there are lots of things that motivate people to work, and working in a shithole isn't one of them.

10

THE FIRST CHOICE of names for our new company was *Deflo*, which was short for "designer floors." Everybody said it looked and sounded weird, so we reversed the order and made it *Flode*. We rented office space in another building that looked like shit, as well it might since it was the former headquarters of the local communist party. Even thirty years later, people who can still remember that era refer to it as such.

As the sales manager, my job was to go to architects and project designers and show them the benefits of having a floor made out of epoxy resin. They are chemically resistant, strong and durable, easy to clean, and cost effective. Czech people are typically slow to innovation, fearing the price and uncertainty, and our first year was tough.

I went wherever I could to drum up orders. In a single day, I did three meetings in Bohemia: one in the north at eight o'clock in the morning, another in the west at one o'clock in the afternoon, and the third one in the south at six in the evening. I covered seven hundred miles between leaving home at dawn and returning at midnight.

Finally, in our second year, we got a huge order for a VIP client at Prague Airport. We delivered everything on time and in the quality and satisfaction that was expected. I later found out that I could have charged them twice the amount they paid and still got the contract, but the most important thing was a positive reference from them. We needed that in order to get new clients.

With business thriving, Kamča and I felt we could afford a house. We found one with half-timber framing under a pitched roof in a part of town that had a very nice village feel to it, yet it was only minutes away from the main square. The owners had recently divorced and the only way the guy could pay off his ex-wife was by selling the house he had built for them. He planned to take what was left over and build a whole new house on a plot he owned not too far away. We offered the asking price and it was ours.

One major hurdle was the 20% down-payment required for the mortgage. We were short even after selling our apartment. A tip led us to a shady broker who knew how to fix it for prospective homeowners like us. He marked up the value of the house so that on paper the loan was for 80% of the sale price when in fact it was for the full price. He seemed to make a lot of money out of business like this, because he later hired us to put in a floor around his indoor swimming pool.

We then did the opposite for the life insurance we needed for the mortgage. We cut the value of the house in half to lower our policy payments. At the time, we were looking at me bringing home a high salary for the next thirty years to pay off the mortgage, only we were barely a fifth of the way there when the first symptoms of ALS appeared.

After a month of remodeling, we moved in in June 2012. Our family had grown by one with the addition of our second son Vincent, who was born on August 4, 2011. His birth was a piece of cake, but the moment he appeared he began screaming his head off. He cried in the hospital, on the way home, in his crib, in our bed. Three-year-old Olda was as laid back as ever, but Vincent needed to be held and comforted constantly.

And then, three months after moving to our new home, something in him snapped. He began crying hysterically, for no apparent reason, and Kamča and I had to take shifts sleeping with him every night. I took the first four hours, she took the second. This went on month after month.

We tried everything to calm him. We changed the colors in his room, rearranged the furniture, basic Feng shui principals of matching energy and environment. We even cast our eyes on the high-voltage transmission lines that run next to our house. I bought a machine to measure the electromagnetic field emitted by them and I remember how nervous we were when we made the first measurement. Would we have to move from our beloved new home? The results showed the emission was and remains perfectly normal.

And just like that it stopped. Vincent was fine, he could sleep by himself. It was March 21, 2013, exactly six months after it started. Since the start date was September 21, we naturally wondered whether the equinox cycle had something to do with it. His distress began on the day darkness begins to outrun the light and it ended on the day light catches up and surpasses darkness. We were again nervous as the next autumn equinox approached, but Vincent then was two years old and in a much calmer state at night.

I turned one of the three rooms that made up our semi-basement into a home office. It soon became my only office and there I worked when I wasn't on the road. Our business had taken off, requiring me to spend more and more time downstairs while my wife and children were above me.

We had to find some balance, so I gave myself home office hours. I was not to start work before eight in the morning and not to work past five in the afternoon. It worked well, but then one night, just after putting the kids to sleep, I went down there just to take care of something really quick.

Of course, it would be quick. It was eight o'clock and I was tired after a full day. So I had at it...and finished at midnight. This happened another night during that week, then another night the next week, until finally it became routine that I worked two nights a week after the kids were asleep. But as with my normal office hours, I set a closing time. At midnight, I turned the computer off and went to bed. It worked well save for those few times I absolutely had to work until two or three in the morning.

Like a lot of people who work long hours, I suppose I

tried to make up for it with family outings and vacations. Every winter we always went to the Alps in Austria or Italy for snowboarding and skiing. Summers were generally spent at home. There are so many mountains, lakes, campsites, bike trails and water parks within an hour of our home that people from Holland, Germany and Poland come here for their vacation.

In 2015, we made our first long trip outside the Czech Republic. The guy who opened the Mattes branch in Hungary had a girlfriend from the south of France. They arranged for us and two other families they knew in Bohemia to come and stay for two weeks in a village next to Saint Tropez. Kamča and I bought a van, a green one, especially for the trip. We loaded up our bikes, bags, kids and dog, and took off.

That was such a nice vacation. We went to Nice, Monaco, and the stunning Verdon Gorge river canyon. The beaches were gorgeous and groomed of litter every night. Unfortunately, that spotlessness spread to the sea life. I went snorkeling one day and didn't see a thing. Not a fish, crab, clam or coral anywhere in sight. Just a sandy bottom.

We had hoped to indulge in fine French cooking while we were there but shelved that plan after our first trip to a restaurant. We expected it to cost more than back home, but four times as much for four times smaller the portion was ridiculous. Instead, we bought local ingredients at the supermarket and tried our hand at French cooking.

On January 25, 2017, our third child was born. From the beginning we wanted three kids, but Kamča miscarried once between Olda and Vincent and we lost another two before our youngest son arrived. Being an easy birth and easygoing infant, Hubert combined the best of both his older brothers.

He was eighteen months old when we went to Turkey for a beach vacation. That's all it was, no sightseeing at all. Never once in my hitchhiking days could I imagine I would one day go somewhere, plant my feet and never move from that spot, but I was now a father of three who worked sixty hours a week. It was great just to lie by the pool or on the beach and consume all the food, desserts and cocktails I wanted.

* * *

In March 2019, Olda was ten, Vincent seven, and Hubert just over two. It was time to put up a swing set in the backyard for our energetic boys. I put it together, but as I started tightening the bolts, I suddenly lost strength in my left hand. Try as I might, I could not grip the wrench tight enough to either push or pull on it. I was now forty-two years old, not the power youth I used to be, but it seemed strange. Since it was cold and windy out that day, I figured I was just chilled to the bone. I went inside, warmed up, and tried again later.

I managed to finish the swing set, but there was clearly something wrong. Although I'm right-handed, my left arm had always been the stronger of the two. I normally used it to lock and unlock doors, but I now found it hard to hold the key between my left thumb and index finger. I couldn't maintain a good grip on the key to turn it in the lock.

The weakness in my left arm and hand persisted, but I could ignore it because it didn't hinder my activities at all. I was still crazy about the mountains and started taking my boys there more. Olda always aimed to please and went along, but Vincent hated walking, much less hiking. He preferred our family outings on bike, with Hubert in the toddler seat behind me.

In the summer, we loaded our bikes into the van and headed to the Alps, first to Austria for four days, then to Slovenia for four days. After that, we spent another four days in Croatia by the beach. It was then, for the first time, that I felt twitching all over my body. I felt it in my legs, in my chest, in my arms, everywhere except above my neck. The worst was my left arm, but I failed to make a connection between it and the weakness I felt there.

In the fall, I went with a group of friends to Poland for some downhill mountain bike riding. It was great fun topped off with beer and roasting sausages around a campfire at night. Suddenly, the twitching in my arm, which had never gone away, became so bad that I felt compelled to show it to the guy next to me. Even in the flickering light he could see that it was something I should have checked out.

Kamča was fearful when I confided in her, not just about the twitching, but also about how I had to rely on my right arm and hand to do most of the steering and braking with my bike. Her training and work in ergotherapy made her familiar with neurodegenerative diseases. She thought they were the worst of all, even worse than cancer, and insisted I see a specialist about it. We decided I would do so after the Christmas holidays.

In January 2020, nine months after the incident with the swing set, I went to see a neurologist who took walk-ins. He noticed something that I didn't, the loss of muscle at the base of my thumb, but he didn't suggest what it might mean. For the weakness in my hand, he diagnosed Carpal Tunnel syndrome, which is caused by a pinched nerve in the wrist. He sent me to an orthopedist, who gave me a shot of corticosteroid. At first, I thought it helped a lot, but it was clearly the placebo effect. My symptoms steadily came back.

In May, I went to our family doctor. She's a really nice person and didn't criticize me at all for waiting so long to seek help, but I could see fear in her eyes. She knew that whatever it was, it was bad. She set up an appointment for me right away with a neurologist who, after testing my strength and reflexes, sent me to Dr. Junkerová, an EMG (electromyography) specialist in Ostrava.

Junkerová inserted a hypodermic needle with electrodes into both of my arms to measure the electrical activity of the muscles when I flexed and relaxed them. It wasn't comfortable but didn't hurt. She brought up the results on her computer and showed me that the wave pattern of my right arm on the screen was fine, but it took a dive on my left arm. I could see with my own eyes that there was something wrong. The doctor nevertheless tried to be reassuring.

"Don't worry, Mr. Slezák. It doesn't have to be it."

It? I didn't know what "it" was supposed to be, so I asked her. That's when she realized that the previous neurologist hadn't briefed me on possible diagnoses or the contents of her report. I had taken the report home with me but didn't have the patience or energy to find out what all the abbreviations meant. Looking at it now, one of them stood clearly out: ALS.

I went home and this time read the report carefully. It was September 2020, eighteen months since I first noticed the weakness in my arm. Never in that time did I consider the possibility that my problem was anything to worry about. Surely it would go away or I could take something or do something to make it go away. I was concerned, yes, but certainly not scared.

Now I was scared. Really scared.

11

I WILL NEVER FORGET how my heart sank reading about amyotrophic lateral sclerosis (ALS) for the first time. For no apparent reason, the motor neurons in our body begin to die. That not only deprives us of our ability to control voluntary movements like walking, talking, eating and breathing, but our muscles waste away without stimulation from the electrical impulses they normally receive from our brains. That's what happened to the muscle in my thumb. The neurons there stopped working, so the muscle withered and vanished. I instantly felt for the muscle in my weakened fingers next to it. Mostly bone. This was bad.

The real terror was reading that there's no cure or any way to slow down or reverse the disease. You're doomed from the moment it starts. It might take two years, five years, even ten years, but you lose in the end. And you know it every step of the way. Other than the psychological stress, your mind is completely healthy the whole time. All you can do is sit there and take it.

It was then that I remembered the ice bucket challenge that swept through the internet a few years earlier. All these people were challenging each other to pour buckets of ice water over their heads to raise awareness of ALS. It was such an obvious publicity stunt that I didn't notice what good cause it was for.

Poor Kamča. Even though the doctor did not diagnose her husband with ALS, he was clearly suffering from a neurological disease that was getting progressively worse. She was devastated and we spent a mostly sleepless night in each other's arms. In the morning, we held it together for the kids. We decided not to say anything to them unless we had to. I refused to let it distract me and went down to my office for another full day of work.

Business as usual became my way of coping. I carried on as if my illness was an inconvenience that I would have sorted out in no time. In a way, that became Kamča's way of coping as well. One of the mainstays of our marriage has been her belief that I can achieve whatever I set out to do. She feels that my mindset, which has lost none of its strength in the face of my weakening body, will help us over this crisis.

I kept reading up on ALS. Incredibly, it was first identified in 1869, more than a hundred and fifty years ago. The most famous person to suffer from it was Stephen Hawking, who survived half a century with it thanks to the round-the-clock medical care he received. In this country, it claimed the life of Stanislav Gross, who became the youngest Czech prime minster in history while I was in America. Kicked out of office on corruption charges, he was forty-three when he was diagnosed with it, the same age as me. He died two years later.

Despite Hawking's profile, no progress was made in his lifetime on finding the cause, much less a cure. Every year sees more and more drugs appear on the market to fight cancer, diabetes, and mental health disorders, but ALS still has science and medicine stumped. The few drugs used to treat it include Riluzole, which is thought to inhibit a neurotransmitter that damages neurons when released in excessive amounts. It also targets a certain protein that disrupts nerve function when it accumulates in clumps.

Riluzole does not reverse the damage already caused by ALS and it extends life by only a few months. Apparently, neurologists recommend it because they have nothing else to offer. Junkerová did not officially diagnose me with ALS, but she recommended I take it just in case.

Since there is no specific medical treatment for my condition, I decided to try various alternative therapies. First, there was *The Journey*, which was developed by an American woman named Brandon Bays. She claimed to have healed a tumor the size of a basketball in her womb in six weeks without any surgery. As the *Journey* therapist in Ostrava explained it to me, the emotional traumas of our childhood are scarred over by time and neglect. These scars form layers around our core, sort of like an onion. Only by peeling away these layers can the healing process begin on a cellular level.

I sat on the couch with my eyes closed as the therapist led me inside my body on a journey into my past. We got as far as my seventh vertebra, but she could not pinpoint the onion. By the end of our next session, the therapist believed the problem was in my previous life, but I told her that's too far back for me to journey in my present condition. I felt we were at a dead end, so I gave it up after that.

Next, I tried special procedures like lymphatic drainage massage, which keeps the lymph fluid balanced throughout the body. It did nothing for me. Finally, I settled into the *Wim Hof Method*. It's a technique that combines breathing exercises, exposure to cold, and mustering willpower for the purpose of reducing stress and improving immunity.

The idea is to increase the level of oxygen in your body and flood it with hormones like adrenaline and cortisone. I would assume a meditative position, begin to artificially hyperventilate and then submerge myself into an ice-cold bath. It's totally brutal, and there are lots of doctors out there who say it's bullshit, but anything was better than nothing.

The reason why Junkerová was unwilling to diagnose me with ALS is because the symptoms were confined to my left hand and arm. She wondered if my problem might be Hirayama disease, which is another neuromuscular disorder that is neither progressive nor fatal and is treatable with intervention. The chances that I had it were slim, however, because it usually strikes in adolescence and it has no connection to the twitching all over my body. Not one but two MRIs dispelled the possibility of Hirayama or any tumors or other abnormalities affecting my nervous system.

I went in twice a year for an EMG, in the spring and fall. In March 2021, two years after my first symptoms, Junkerová told me that whatever disease I had, it couldn't be ALS. It was progressing too slowly. She couldn't rule it out, but she was hopeful to the point of suggesting that I could stop taking Riluzole if I wished. That I did, because this drug doesn't improve the quality of life with ALS. It only makes you suffer with it a few months longer.

Kamča was thrilled with the news, but privately I wasn't sure. We went to Croatia for our summer vacation and it was then, for the first time, that I felt weakness in my right hand. Instinctively, I kept picking up things and gripping them to test my diminishing strength. Kamča noticed and together we exchanged one of the most doleful and heartbreaking glances you can imagine.

When we got home, she fell back on what Junkerová said, but I told her I know what I feel and it wasn't good. Sure enough, my EMG in September confirmed that my right arm was starting to fail as well. There was no denying it anymore. I had ALS and it was progressing, slowly perhaps but steadily.

For two and a half years, we eluded the dreaded diagnosis. Kamča cried and cried and I comforted her. In our desperation and frustration, we talked more and more about possible causes. If we could just figure that out, if we could identify what was hiding in plain sight, we had a chance. There were the usual vices. I used to smoke, both cigarettes and weed, and I have drunk a fair amount of alcohol, but my lean diet, lots of exercise and fresh mountain air had to have neutralized their effects.

Snowboarding certainly took a physical toll on me. When I came back from America, two of my middle ribs on the left side kept popping out of joint, and I needed Kamča to walk on my back to pop them back in. I didn't find relief for this problem until I took up yoga. It worked so well that I continued to do yoga after my ribs healed.

I found an instructor in Marcela, my childhood friend and former neighbor. She and Marek had had another daughter, moved to a bigger apartment, and got married after fifteen years of living together. In that time, she took up yoga and became an instructor as part of her search for self-improvement.

That was a period when Kamča and I began nurturing a strong spiritual presence in our lives. We looked into the mysteries of energies and multiple dimensions. She turned the room in the basement next door to mine into her own home office to provide massages to her growing list of clientele. She infused it with incense, music and carefully arranged objects and pictures.

I love that place, and not just for her massages. I feel so much at peace with the world in there that it's possible the progress of my ALS has been slow precisely because of my spiritual wellbeing. But that inevitably took a hit after the disease reached a point where I could no longer do power yoga. I switched to a slower form, but the complete loss of motor functions in my left arm and hand forced me to give up yoga altogether.

Now that my diagnosis was official, I had to completely change my attitude about ALS. I remember early on reading an article that said the first step in treatment was to like the disease, and if not that, to at least accept it. I thought, "No way." Liking it was out of the question. Who could like such a horrible fate?

But ignoring it was no longer an option. It's foolish to pretend nothing is happening to you when you know it's ravaging your body every day and night. Not just the loss of movement and all the twitching, but seeing yourself shrink as your muscles shrivel up. Other people, moreover, were beginning to notice my increasingly gaunt appearance and my left arm just dangling there. It was time to come clean and admit to the world that I had ALS.

12

FOR MORE THAN TWO YEARS, I was able to keep my family and friends in the dark about my illness. When we met up for birthdays, Christmases, regular gatherings or outings and someone noticed the twitching or trouble I was having with my left arm, I told them the truth. I had a motor neuron disorder, but we weren't sure which one. After the diagnosis was clear and they asked or alluded to it, I told them it was ALS. I didn't add anything about the grim prospects for recovery, only that I'm convinced I'm going to beat it.

Even now, I can't remember the first time we told the children about it. In fact, we never said anything to Hubert. Since he was just over two years old when my first

symptoms appeared, he has no memory of me ever using my left arm and hand. He's now six and knows my condition is not getting better, but it's all he's ever known, so we leave it at that.

With Vincent, I remember we were in Prague visiting friends and he was sitting on my lap. He could feel the twitching in my thighs and asked me about it. After I explained what it meant, he asked me if I might end up in a wheelchair. I told him I hoped not, but it was a possibility, and if it came to that, it would mean a big change in our lives, starting with modifying our home. It's been more than a year since then and I can still walk up and down our stairs, but just recently he asked me again about the wheelchair.

Olda was thirteen when one day he asked me if I had ALS. I don't know where he heard about it or if he figured it out for himself online. As with the adults, I only told him that I had something similar to it. It was maybe a year later that I told him I had it. He didn't show any reaction. Being kids, he and his brother take bad news in stride. They see me, as their father, as someone who is strong and capable of dealing with adversity like this.

Otherwise, my two older sons are so different from each other. Olda is always on time, always finishes everything he starts. His dream is to study in the United States on the Future Leaders Exchange Program, or FLEX. He talks about living in Los Angeles someday, which I can't understand when you've got San Diego just down the coast.

Then there's Vincent. That boy has a million projects, never finishes any of them. If you send him off to do something, you can bet you'll find him doing something completely different. He's late for everything because he has no concept of time, but ALS is changing that. Now he's very conscious of time as I become more incapacitated. He misses our bike rides together and games of ping pong and horsing around. I sense that it makes him angry at times, understandably so.

Actually, I continued snowboarding all this time. In the winter of 2022, three years since I first saw a doctor about my condition, we went to Poland for the school break. In four days, I covered sixty miles with my snowboard. It was a good experience, and the only help I needed was with

unsnapping my boots from my board and getting my coat, gloves and boots on and off.

This past winter, however, it was miserable. We again went to Poland, but this time I could only manage three runs downhill and nine miles total. Not only has the loss of muscle in my calves made it harder for me to control the board, but the loss of mass throughout my body has deprived me of a natural cushion. I fell three times from the standing position and each time was really painful. Because I don't have enough strength in my neck to stiffen up before impact, my head hit the snow like whiplash. Add to that the exhaustion I feel from any physical exertion, as well as the fear that someone might crash into me on the slope, and I decided to give up snowboarding until I get better.

I also kept on biking. I found a way to cope with it by having my right handlebar fitted with both the rear and front brakes, and by wearing a brace on my left wrist strapped to that side of the handlebar. But this year I gave it up because it's become too dangerous. If I fall, I will more than likely break a bone.

There's also the joy that's no longer there. Riding a bike or snowboard has always been an exhilarating experience. The wind in your face, the trees, the mountains and the endless parade of nature before you. The last time I rode, however, I was endlessly vigilant to ensure I posed no danger to myself or others. It left me mentally and physically exhausted.

Even my beloved excursions in the mountains have come to an end. I used to do this thing where every Saturday morning at six o'clock, I would hike up to the top of Lysá hora as fast as possible, then jog down and finish it off with a cold bath in the stream. I would come home around nine o'clock, just as my family was getting up, and together we had breakfast on the terrace.

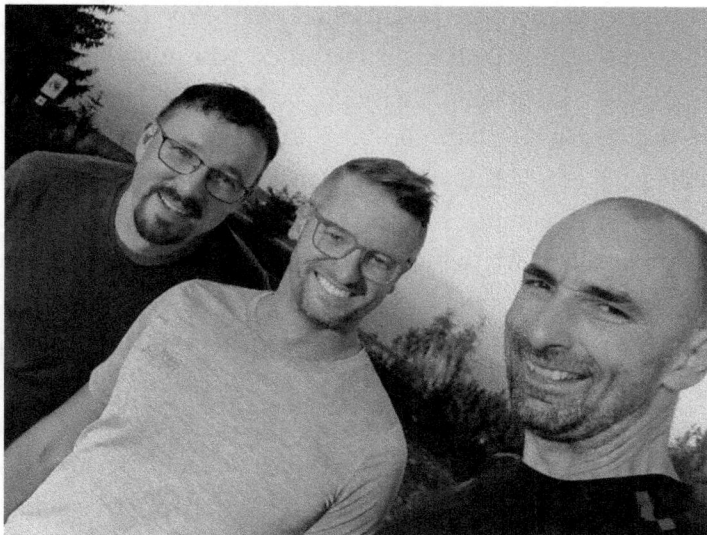

My friends Michal Štefek and Zbyněk Majer often joined me on these jaunts, but Štefek hates getting up early and preferred the excursions we did at night. We would get to the top late in the afternoon, have a few beers in the pub, watch the indescribably beautiful sunset, then head down with headlamps guiding our way. It seems dangerous, but we knew these trails like the back of our hands. It was fun and joy all the way.

Now, just a few weeks ago, we went to the top of a hill with a walking distance of just over a mile. The weather was radiant and the gradient barely noticeable, but it took me forever because of all the stops I had to make. I have nevertheless come to appreciate a slower pace. Relax more, enjoy the moment more, forget this macho drive to push myself to extremes in the belief that a tough body is a healthy one. Today, I'm only a shadow of that super fit and lean guy who used to race up and down the mountain.

Some of this realization has to do with my whole new approach to breathing. I gave up the *Wim Hof Method* after a year because it had no effect on the disease as far as I could tell. Around that time, Kamča heard this guy on TV talk about breathing. His name is Rostislav Václavek and he developed his own therapeutic method for wellbeing. We set up an appointment to meet him.

He explained to us the concepts of the sympathetic and parasympathetic nervous systems, where the first one gears us up for fight or flight, and the second one for rest and digest. In sympathetic, we breathe through our mouths because we need extra oxygen. In parasympathetic, we do it through our nose because we don't. By regularly breathing through our mouths, as I've done all my whole life, we feed a constant state of stress, which is at the core of many diseases.

It made a lot of sense. He told me I should cut out all thoughts of macho, ego-driven therapies. Take everything slowly, easily, breathing only through my nose the whole time. I left his office and climbed Lysá hora that very day. It took me ninety minutes, which is twice what I previously aimed for but still faster than what ordinary people without a disability can manage. That convinced me and eventually I attended some of his courses, including intermittent fasting and core stability.

Václavek had been a Wim Hof disciple before deciding he could do it better, including adopting *Oxygen Advantage* as his breathing technique. It was developed by Patrick Mckeown, a really nice Irish guy who's boring compared to the animated Wim Hof. Basically, it's about learning how not to breathe so often. You train yourself to wait after you

exhale. That increases your tolerance to carbon dioxide, which reduces your need to inhale. This allows you to better regulate the oxygen inside your body.

Some people become stressed out by breathing less than what they are used to, but I quickly mastered it. I decided to take it even further and become a certified instructor through an online course. As an instructor, I was expected to seek out athletes to show them how breathing with this technique will improve their performance, but my focus was on people with ALS.

It's a well-known fact that most sufferers die because they lose the ability to breathe. That came up in a recent webinar sponsored by ALSA, the ALS Association. The speaker encouraged those in attendance to work on developing their lung power because they were going to need it later on. The method he offered, however, involved putting an apparatus in their mouths, which is already wrong because we should be breathing through our noses.

I spoke up and told everyone that I was still breathing on my own after four years of ALS in part thanks to *Oxygen Advantage*. The ALSA representative suddenly exclaimed that she had just taken the same course and it persuaded her that it was something their association should pursue further. They would contact me shortly about it, she said.

ALSA is a great association. They help sufferers get equipment and provide subsidies for speech therapy and other forms of assistance. They also offer legal advice, which is important for prodding the authorities into action. Czech bureaucracy is notoriously slow and makes no exceptions for people racing against the clock. In one well publicized case, it took the government so long to approve a wheelchair for one sufferer that by the time it arrived he needed a completely different wheelchair.

Lucky for me, the social security taxes I paid in America entitled me to disability benefits from there. I made the application and the next day the money was in my account. Bu contrast, the Czech government takes up to ninety days to approve your application for benefits. Three months is a lifetime for an ALS patients. In that time, you can go from walking, talking and breathing on your own to being bedridden with an apparatus by your side.

The bureaucrats haven't changed their ways, but I have finally changed mine. I avoided ALSA and their webinars for the longest time. It was part of my pretense that I didn't have the disease. Then one day, Michal Štefek told me to stop playing games and get with the program. He was right, but truth be told, I just couldn't bear to see other sufferers sitting there online in physically debilitated condition. The image haunted me.

But now I have a new outlook on everything. If science and medicine are unable to help us, then at least we can help each other. My intervention during the webinar has perhaps given other ALS patients new hope and quality of life. With that comes spiritual rejuvenation, which offers more substance than all this talk about liking this terrible disease.

Those listening on the other end would have noted the fact that my own struggle has been going on for more than four years. That's a long time with ALS. I can't say for sure how much all the therapies I've tried have contributed to it and my feeling of wellbeing in general, but I know I would never have come this far without Kamča by my side.

The beautiful girl I married fifteen years ago has lost none of her sense of fun and adventure, but her strength and will of purpose in the face of this adversity has been nothing less than amazing. She has picked up all the slack created by my inability to work full time or be a full-time father for that matter. She is quite simply everything I could ever hope for in the woman to share my life with. It has always been a measure of our love that we never celebrate our wedding day as our anniversary, rather the first night we held each other in our arms.

In October 2022, we reaffirmed that love with a trip for just the two of us. We went to the Greek island of Santorini, which is famous for its whitewashed houses overlooking the sea. The weather, food, people, everything was as pristine and perfect as the water below. It was a week full of passion and pleasure on an island paradise, but if truth be told, there was also a hint of fear and sadness. We came home emotionally uplifted and drained at the same time.

13

GOING BACK A YEAR to May 2022, Václavek organized a weekend workshop on cold-water therapy, which he does differently from Wim Hof. Kamča joined me, and while there, we met a very nice lady who told us about some liquid drops that are supposed to have a special curative effect. She said that they contain not only herbs, but information. You pour a few drops on your skin, rub them in, and they know what to do.

It sounded completely off the wall, but she explained to us that everything is energy in the form of waves and vibrations, something like quantum physics. We see and feel everything as three-dimensional objects, but when you get beyond that limitation and think of everything as energy, then you can understand how something like drops, which is also waves and vibrations at its core, could actually have information to convey to our body cells.

It proved another dead end, but the lady really wanted to help me, that much I was sure of. She told me I should listen to Joe Dispenza, whom my friend Marcela also recommended. Like Brandon Bays, Dispenza also claims to have avoided surgery by using his mind. He was in a cycling accident that left him with six compressed vertebrae in his spine. The combination of cycling and the spine, where ALS degeneration is first prominent, was enough to capture my attention.

His theory, as I understand it, is that real change in life

only exists outside of three dimensions. Just because something cannot be healed physically doesn't mean it cannot be healed at all. You have to connect to the quantum field, which is done through meditation. Right now, our brainwaves are in high beta, middle beta or low beta on the spectrum. From beta, you have to get to alpha, and from alpha to theta, and finally to delta.

Essentially, you're getting mellower with each step, until finally you're in the deep sleep state. The trick is to reach gamma, which is the state of sub-consciousness. That puts you in the quantum field, where, because time doesn't exist, you can seek out whatever afflicts you and heal it at the core.

I had already started meditation with Václavek because it's a good way to slow yourself down. With Dispenza, I listen to his reverberating tones two times a day, half an hour in the morning and half an hour in the afternoon. I'm always sitting, because if I lie down, I'll fall asleep. I can't say I have reached my sub-conscious, however. The problem I have is the twitching.

It used to be only bad when I was tired, but now the twitching goes on all day and night. It's like a fly constantly buzzing around you, which is terrible when you're trying to concentrate. But bad as it is for meditation, it's a nightmare for sleeping. Putting a pillow between my arm and body has allowed me to isolate the nerve-wracking movement at the source, but I can still feel it in my head, like having a throbbing headache. Twitching, twitching, twitching, non-stop twitching.

For our summer vacation of 2022, we decided to switch directions and go north to Poland. I have a habit of thinking every vacation is absolutely the best, but this one really was special. We covered 1,700 miles in our van, plus countless more by foot, bike and boat. The cities, parks, lakes and trails of Poland are still a relatively unknown treasure in this part of the world. A real gem is Łeba on the Baltic Sea, with its big, beautiful dunes of white sand. The water is certainly colder than in Hawaii but there are no hotels or condos on the beach to cramp you or spoil the view. Michal Štefek, his wife Lenka and their two girls joined us, along with other longtime family friends Zbyněk and Petra Majer and their daughter.

In February 2023 I went back to Poland, to Warsaw specifically, for one of Dispenza's retreats. There were fifteen hundred people there, and from what I could tell, most were healthy. They probably had other issues like family and careers. It started with Dispenza asking us to wish for four things to happen. My first was to have my neurons repaired. Second was to repair my muscles. Third, no more twitching. And fourth, no more muscle cramps, which hit me most often in my legs.

We were then asked to write down a list of elevated emotions. I had to do it in my head because I can no longer write with the fingers on my right hand, only use my index finger to poke and swipe. My emotions were joy, gratitude, freedom from my condition, and pride in the sense that I will be very proud of myself when I beat this thing.

After that, Dispenza led us into meditation, and I swear, I did it. I connected to the quantum field! It's possible that all that energy pooled into one room helped me reach it, but what did it matter? It felt absolutely amazing. Marcela was with me and she said she felt the same thing. We looked at each other, completely unaware of time. Were we there for five minutes, ten minutes, an hour? Neither of us had any clue.

It's only in the quantum field that your brainwaves can achieve coherency, which is vital for manifesting your wish list of elevated emotions. This is not so hard as it sounds. You can fool the brain into believing anything, which is what makes ordinary marketing and propaganda so effective. All you have to do is imagine your future in a state of elevated emotions, and then maintain it.

The person I see in five years is the same person I was five years ago. The former me as the future me is simply bringing the past forward. I impose my formerly healthy body on my currently diseased body. In a few years' time, it will be like I never had ALS.

I met a woman here who successfully achieved this. She's forty, about my age now, and suffered from a type of sclerosis that had no cure. It left her bedridden and incontinent and feeling sorry for herself all the time. She was put in touch with a healer who said the cause of her illness was her habit of always trying to please everyone. When the others didn't reciprocate, resentment built up inside her, poisoning her spiritually and drowning her in a deep state of victimhood. She had to swear off that type of behavior.

The second thing is, she had to imagine the future that she wanted, then live that life in her thoughts with emotion. She did it intensively, imagining the smell of the ocean and feeling the wind in her hair on the beach. It lasted for ten years, but she's completely healthy today, walking, running, taking care of three dogs.

She couldn't believe it herself and asked for a brain scan. The neurologist was shocked to see that she had the brainwaves of a fourteen-year-old girl. I don't need to go that far back in my life, but if it takes me ten years to be able to walk on the beach again with my wife and boys, I'm all up for it.

This is where epigenetic science comes in. It's the idea that our genes can be manipulated in real time. I have to convince my brain that my left arm and hand are working properly. If I can do that, then an unconscious process to repair them will start. The faulty production of proteins and enzymes, which is thought to be the root cause of ALS, will sort itself out. That's the physical manifestation of the healing process.

It's second nature for science and medicine to doubt and criticize these therapies, but here's the thing: If I get cancer, the medical establishment will offer me treatment. It could be surgery, chemotherapy, radiation, pills or injections. I've got ALS instead, and what do they offer? Nothing. No answers, no explanations, no treatments. That's hard to live with. So, to the critics and doubters of alternative therapies, I say offer me something first, then we'll talk about these other guys.

But just as I'm not afraid to try something new, I will also give it up if it fails to produce results. I can't say I got nothing out of *The Journey* and *Wim Hof*, but not enough to convince me they were working. On the other hand, the timelessness of quantum energy seems to be working, so I will stick with it for the time being (no pun intended).

There is still Riluzole, but I didn't see the point of taking it again for so little potential benefit. But as I'm speaking now, the FDA has fast-tracked a new drug that provides treatment for SOD1-ALS, which involves the mutation of the SOD1 gene. It hasn't been approved in the European Union, but a friend of mine in America says he knows how to get it for me.

Of course, I will speak to my doctor first. I read that only 2% of ALS sufferers have this mutation. The unlikelihood that I have it only further underscores the lack of treatment available from the professionals. As they say, with ALS there is no treatment, only care.

14

AT THE BEGINNING of May 2023, we heard an unconfirmed report that five people had been cured of ALS. The cause of the disease was not a protein, rather an animal-borne parasite. All this came about after a friend of mine put my story online and a healer named Adam saw it. He contacted me and introduced me to the work of Hana Blahová, whose treatment of ALS patients had been unsuccessful until she realized that the question isn't what ALS is, but where it is. She now believes that a parasitic worm carried by foxes somehow finds its way to our nerve centers above the spinal cord.

That could definitely be my case. Our adored Labrador Benny, who died two years ago at the age of fourteen, loved to eat shit. Whatever he came across during our hikes in the woods, he gobbled up. It's possible he had ingested this parasite in this manner and passed it on to me. Only by finding and killing it can my neurons and muscles begin to regenerate. But the worrisome news is that the symptoms usually don't appear for more than ten years after the infection sets in, and the prognosis is that, once the parasite is gone, it will take at least another ten years for my body to heal afterwards.

This information reached me just as Dispenza was organizing another retreat, this time in Vienna. I was eager to go. Once registration opened, I began typing away with the little movement I have left in the fingers on my right hand. I was still typing fourteen minutes later when registration closed. The retreat was already booked up despite the $2,300 admission fee.

To me, it was another sign that it's time to move on. Lately, in my morning meditations, I have felt as if I was really inside my body, trying to clean it of the protein long thought to be the cause of this disease. When I came out of it, I was miserable and nauseous because I was unable to do it alone. I need someone to help me, and suddenly, out of nowhere, Adam appears.

Kamča and I met him in Brno, and he told us that based on my symptoms, the parasite was affecting eight of my twelve nerve centers. I already had four MRIs during the course of my illness and not one of them showed any sign of cysts to indicate the presence of parasites in the body. But truth be told, the doctors weren't looking for any, either.

Adam recommended that I start taking a drug called Praziquantel. Because it's not approved here, the only way to get it is through the black market. I have to say that Praziquantel has taken a toll on me. Whereas I have always slept fairly well even with ALS, now I wake up at night and find it hard to go back to sleep. All I can do is get up and read something or play a game on my phone. My appetite has also been good this whole time, but not lately, and that's causing me to lose even more weight. But I look at the loss of sleep and appetite as evidence that the drug is helping my body get rid of the parasite.

Later in May, I flew with some friends to Amsterdam to spend a couple of days on a houseboat. This was something Igor and I arranged last year, but at the last minute, work commitments prevented him from going. Because I was taking the new drug, I abstained from any smoking, especially weed, and I kept my drinking to a minimal. I had a great time, remembering all the wonderful memories of my visits to Holland.

I felt good and optimistic when I came home. Kamča and I went to Brno for a check-up, and Adam pronounced that all but one of my nerve centers was free of the parasite. It seems, then, that I have the physical cause of my ALS finally under control. And the same goes with the spiritual cause.

That came about when a friend of mine put me in touch with another healer who's really out there. He's this guy who uses meditation to connect to space, where he devises a mantra for you. You use the mantra to send energy back to space, and this results in forgiveness for all the people, including yourself, who are responsible for whatever illness you. After that, the healing process begins.

The interesting thing here is, he noticed how the left side of my body is more affected than my right. I'm actually not surprised by it at all. There has always been an imbalance in my body. The left side had always been the stronger of the two, and even my left foot is one shoe size bigger than my right.

This healer said the left side of our bodies is the more feminine side, and the right one the more masculine side. He took that as a sign that I have a problem with women. When I told this to Silvie, my physical therapist at the health clinic, she said that she always thought it was the opposite. Left is more masculine, right more feminine.

When the healer heard that, he insisted he was right the

first time around, but he added that, after further consultation with space, I didn't have a problem with women after all. It turned out to be a false alarm, but whether he knew it or not, he was on to something. I found this out from the next healer, whose name is Lucie.

Lucie had a freak accident as a kid that cost her an eye. In trying to understand how it happened to her and why, she gained insight into the mysteries of fate, which she continues with card-reading and numerology. I can't say it's something that I put a lot of faith in, but I listened to her and she came to the conclusion that I'm an A-35 type karma healer. That means it's my responsibility to see to the wellbeing of my tribe or family.

Here I failed. My mother sucked all the energy out of the men in our family, making them submissive and harmless. My father was always too afraid to go out and have a beer with me for fear of her disapproval, and my brother is fifty and still all alone. No family, no relationship. As a karma healer, I could have fixed all that, but instead I ran away.

Looking at the numbers, Lucie saw a strong connection between me and my mother. When I told her that I always tried to keep my distance from her, she told me that was wrong. The connection I have with my mother is the same that I have with mother earth. If the connection between us is weak, it means I'm not firmly anchored to the ground and therefore I'm not receiving all the natural energy that I need.

For proof, she advised me to contact this guy who runs *Constellations*, which is a therapeutic exercise designed to get at the core of family problems. Oh, great, I thought, another journey in search of the trauma onion. I listened to her with weariness until she mentioned that the exercise was run by Hynek, my old classmate who later became a high school teacher with a passion for martial arts and mysticism. I called and arranged a session with him.

It was almost thirty years ago that Hynek and I were the only members of our school trip to Holland who dived into the cold North Sea. Unlike me, he had the strength in our gymnastics class to master the rings. He's still strong, energetic, and talks a million miles an hour. I can only imagine what he must have thought when he saw me with my wasted body, now struggling to put even basic sentences together.

The exercise consisted of me calling up other attendees and arranging them as a sort of constellation representing my family dynamic. These strangers knew nothing about me beforehand, but I'll be damned if they didn't have the relationship between me, my parents and my brother pegged. They really opened up my eyes to a lot of things I never considered before.

For example, when I left for America, my mother wanted to come with me. She wanted to go somewhere too because she was deeply unhappy. She had a rough childhood being the only daughter born to middle-aged parents, whose older children were high-achievers. All she ever thought about was escape, which is what led her to being picked up by my father on the road that day. My mother felt that by going to America, I abandoned her.

You might say our relationship never recovered. She hated all my girlfriends, Lenka especially. So strained were things between us that she was one of the last people I told about my illness. I now realize that was a mistake. You can't begin to heal unless you forgive, and that, I can say, I have done. Now, everything has changed. I feel a closeness between me and my parents and brother that never existed before, that I never thought was possible to achieve. I suppose that's to be expected under these conditions, but healing the rift in my family reinforces my belief that ALS can be overcome too.

During our session, I told Lucie about my earlier bout with sarcoidosis. It's an illness that never goes away and yet somehow I beat it. She interpreted that as me cheating fate. I didn't suffer from it as I was meant to. I'm not sure I buy that, but the numbers told her that my earthly cycle is coming up for renewal on February 9, 2024, when I turn 47. She told me anything can happen until then, which was a roundabout way of saying that my body will either die or be on the road to rejuvenation.

I'm positive it's going to be the latter. I have discovered the physical and spiritual cause of my ALS and both are undergoing the healing process. Now I need to work on recovery. The disease has devastated my body, has robbed me of millions, if not billions of neurons and muscle fibers. Left to natural growth, it could take years, even decades, and I don't want my children to spend their entire childhood with this thing hanging over them. I need energy to speed up my recovery, and the place to get it, as I found out in spring, is in Bosnia.

There's a cluster of hills north of Sarajevo that looks like pyramids. Now covered with trees, there are claims that they were built by ancient Illyrians. These pyramids are famous for having tunnels that concentrate enormous amounts of energy. If I can harvest that energy, it will put me firmly on the road to recovery in time for my new life cycle, which is a little over seven months away.

Since I'm in no condition to go there alone, I asked Michal Štefek to come with me. In February, he broke a thigh bone in a skiing accident in the Italian Alps. The bone did not heal as quickly as the doctors had hoped, so he could benefit from some extra natural energy as well. I told him we're going to Montenegro for our vacation this summer. We will stop at the pyramids on our way there, check out the tunnels, and if the prospects look good, he and I can go there sometime after we get back.

Kamča is understandably concerned. I'm skin and bones, my breathing is worse, and my speaking and swallowing get more agonizing every day. I'm only able to swallow water when it's thickened with something first. I need Kamča to cut up my meals for me, which I can eat alone only by using a brace on my arm. She thinks we should go to Poland or somewhere close on vacation, but I'm convinced that I need a booster to kick-start my recovery, and these pyramids look like it.

The highest of them certainly has the shape of a pyramid, and the name given to it, the Pyramid of the Sun, is a good sign. It reminds me of my hundreds of treks up and down Lysá hora, where I always stopped to take in the sunset or sunrise. Bathing in the new rays and old rays of the day's sunlight filled me with energy. My only regret is that I didn't conserve that energy deep in my core instead of wasting it on some macho sprint up and down the mountain.

That extra energy would come in handy now as I continue to meditate and work on achieving a state of elevated emotion. In a sense, I feel I have achieved it as far as joy and gratitude are concerned. For example, we have a favorite spot in the mountains where we go camping. We bring our bikes there, ride the trails, enjoy dinner around the campfire, then fall blissfully asleep with two of us in the van and three in the tent.

It's absolute heaven, and because we do it every year, it never really changes. Every year is the same as the year before it and year after it, as if time has stopped in our lives in that one place. There's no past or future, only the present, a beautiful, magical moment of me, my wife and children together, riding our bikes, rolling in the grass, laughing ourselves to sleep.

I can still feel that joy in my mind. Even if I'm wrong and I never get to feel it again in my body, I'll always be eternally grateful that I have them and everything else in my life. I may not look like it, but I truly feel like the luckiest guy in the world.

AFTERWORD

From March to May 2023, I had six conversations with Michal, each lasting about two hours. The last one ended on his hopeful news of the possible cause of his ALS and the new drug he was taking. "Things are happening," he said confidently. And then, just over a month later, he appeared in a local documentary marking ALS Day, which occurs on June 21st. He looked tired and listless, worryingly so. I arranged to visit him a week after the broadcast.

In our previous conversations, he always met me at the door and led me down to his basement office. This time, he sat in the corner of the living room couch and didn't move from it until I left an hour later. He spoke clearly but with an air of fatigue and he had trouble swallowing, but he remained optimistic as he updated me on his current

therapies and plans to go to the Bosnian pyramids. We agreed to meet again after his return in early August.

In the first week of July, he and his family, plus Kamča's sister Karolína and her husband Jonáš, packed up their green van and left on vacation. They stopped in Visoko, just northwest of Sarajevo, and joined throngs of other tourists to get into the pyramid tunnels. Kamča maintained an open mind about it, but they had gone through so many therapies that she couldn't help but feel apathetic over another one. She got nothing from the tunnels, but Olda felt a distinct tingling in his legs, and Vincent's constantly congested nose was suddenly clear. Michal left convinced that he had to come back and do it for real.

The next day, they continued to Montenegro. Their accommodation was dumpy, the sea placid and full of algae, and they could only get to it by climbing up and down steps, which was hard for Michal. Otherwise, he was happy there, doing meditation on the beach and being in the water alone with his thoughts. His spirits were further lifted by the arrival of four friends, two couples who had come to Bosnia in RVs to ride their dirt bikes.

Out of nowhere, Michal came up with the idea that they should rent a boat and spend the day further out on the water. The sea there was indescribably beautiful and they had great fun swimming around the boat. Michal didn't go into the water, rather sat at the front of the boat with that grin of his and enjoyed the good time had by all.

When they got home after a week, he went straight to bed and was mostly quiet after that. All food to him now smelled horrible and tasted like plastic. Much to Kamča's dismay, he insisted on driving himself to his appointment with the acupuncturist. The next day he drove himself for his rehabilitation with Silvie, but came home and said that that was it, he was through with driving.

He busied himself with his trip to Bosnia despite the signs that he was growing weaker every day. His plan was to go with Michal Štefek and Jonáš, but his mother-in-law, Alča, who was helping with his care, offered to go with them and Kamča insisted on it. Štefek, called "Štefais" by his friends, had not seen Michal for a month and was surprised by his condition. It took Michal twenty seconds or more to say something and then it was not entirely coherent. They left at seven in the morning on Saturday, July 29th, in the green van and arrived twelve hours later in Visoko. They took possession of the house Michal had rented online, a luxurious dwelling that was only a five-minute walk from the entrance to the pyramid.

They intended to stay there until the following Saturday. The two Michals would visit the tunnels every day in search of healing power. Like Jonáš, Štefais brought his laptop in order to work remotely during that week. That meant he had to get up early in the morning to go to the tunnels. He thought his friend would be happy to hear that, because Michal had always pushed him to get up early for their treks to the mountains. But now he only looked at him and said, with perfect irony and greatly improved articulation, "I've started sleeping in lately."

They went to the pyramid in the morning. It was only sixty yards from the parking lot to the entrance, but Michal needed to stop just before they reached it in order to catch his breath. They made sure he was warm because it's only 54°F (12°C) in there. They spent an hour inside, with Michal by himself in one of the side rooms doing his meditation.

When they came out, he suggested they have coffee at one of the outdoor cafés. His sense of perception was as sharp as ever. There were two stray dogs playing nearby and Michal noticed that one of them had an injury on its paw, which turned out to be the case.

They went back to the house and Michal took a nap. Later in the afternoon, Štefais went to the tunnels by himself because Michal said he was really tired, but upon returning, Štefais learned that the other three had also gone there after him. Michal had suddenly stood up and told his in-laws, "Let's go to the tunnels." They were now sitting on the porch and Michal was in a very animated mood. He said he had successfully reached the quantum field on that second visit.

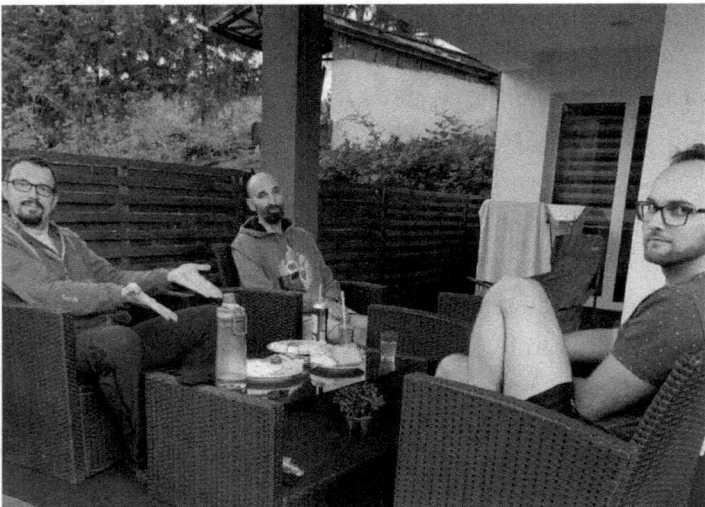

He did it, moreover, on his own, without guided tones in his headphones. His speech was much better, he had an appetite and suggested they all go out for dinner while they were there. "The Bosnians really know how to prepare lamb," he said. By this point, he was unable to eat on his own because his right hand had very little grip left, but the feeling around the table was one of optimism. His energy level had risen remarkably after that second visit to the Ravne Tunnels.

The next day was a Monday. Since Štefais had an online meeting at nine, he got up at seven-thirty to be at the tunnels when they opened at eight. Seeing him leave, Michal said he admired him for getting up so early. It was another nostalgic dig at their friendship of thirty years, where the only real point of contention had always been what time to start the day's adventure in the mountains. Michal had breakfast with Alča and Jonáš and later that morning they took him to the tunnels.

The plan was for all four of them to go to the tunnels again late in the afternoon. Michal was already tired by then, and seeing how much difficulty he had had walking to the entrance, they proposed getting him a wheelchair. He was steadfastly against it. He had always been that way. When he found out that his family was looking into getting him an electric wheelchair, he got angry and resentful, and he absolutely refused to discuss a tracheotomy to help him breathe easier.

Only in this case, he had no choice about the wheelchair. The tunnels closed at seven and the parking lot was chaos with cars maneuvering about. They had to move fast if

Michal hoped to reach the quantum field, or "white space" as they dubbed it, that day. Štefais ran to the entrance, bought the tickets, got the wheelchair, and they helped a reluctant Michal sit in it.

They rolled him to his usual spot in the tunnels. Štefais went to his spot, and Alča and Jonáš passed the time in the souvenir shops outside. After the tunnels closed, they found a café that was still open and ordered ice coffees. Michal was quiet but he was following the conversation with his eyes. When he tried to talk, it was only mumbling and the others strained to understand him.

They went back to the house for a light dinner of cold cuts and vegetables. Michal's appetite was good and he indicated to Štefais to keep piling the morsels of ham, tomatoes and cheese into his mouth. At nine o'clock, he went to bed. Štefais sat on the side of it and asked him if his meditation in the tunnels that day had been good. Michal indicated that it wasn't. Was he still satisfied they came? He indicated he was. Štefais told him that tomorrow they would use the wheelchair so Michal could save his strength for his meditation. He agreed.

Michal went to sleep, and Štefais joined Alča and Jonáš on the porch. They saw the moon rising above the pyramid. The actual full moon was to occur the next night, but it was a supermoon and already very bright. They went to bed, with Štefais and Jonáš in their respective rooms, while Alča shared a room with Michal. He was sound asleep.

Štefais got up early the next morning for his trek to the tunnels. At 7:40, Alča appeared and wished him luck. At 7:51, he got up from the porch to leave when Alča told him that Michal wasn't breathing. Štefais followed her into the bedroom and felt his arm and forehead. They were cold. Michal had died in his sleep during the early morning hours of August 1st. His death was later determined to have occurred between three and four o'clock, as the supermoon descended in the sky opposite the Pyramid of the Sun.

That morning Kamča took their youngest son Hubert to his daycare center. It was already arranged for a friend to pick him up later that day and he would stay the night with them. As she got in her car to leave the center, her phone rang and "Mamka" (Mom) appeared on the screen. She knew immediately.

At home, she was consoled by her sisters Karolína and Alena and by Štefais's wife Lenka. Olda and Vincent were at a summer camp two hours away by car. A family friend named "Santi", who went with Michal to Holland and had dropped by to visit them in Montenegro, drove her there that morning. She summoned the boys to a tent and told them she had bad news for them. Their father has died. There were tears, but no crying. They had all gone on the belief that Michal would get well one day, but also talked about the possibility that he wouldn't. It was much the same when she told Hubert after he came home.

In Visoko, Štefais called Malik, the owner of the house. A former professional handball player, he lived many years in Northern Cyprus, spoke excellent English and was well-connected. His mother was the vice-mayor, his father-in-law the chief of police. He managed all the calls they needed to make.

First two policemen arrived, the younger one speaking English, then a detective and forensic specialist. All agreed it was a case of natural death, so there was no need for an "abduction" as they kept saying, but obviously meaning autopsy. After that two men in street clothes, driving an unmarked van, arrived to take Michal to the morgue.

The coroner listed the cause of death as a heart attack, but lots of ALS patients die in their sleep from the carbon dioxide that builds up in their blood as a result of their breathing difficulties. Malik and his wife, who were helpful throughout, came over later in the afternoon with baskets of food. That night, Štefais, Alča and Jonáš watched the full supermoon rise over the pyramid and couldn't help but see it as a sign.

It took the insurance company five days to approve the repatriation of his body, because for some reason death by ALS required special authorization. Two companies took care of the repatriation. The three Czech visitors then got into the green van for the twelve-hour journey home. They left on Saturday, as originally planned.

I already knew of Michal's passing. Štefais, who used to be my student, sent me a message from Bosnia the day after. I had also seen the full supermoon the evening before, rising above Lysá hora. I remember thinking Michal would have loved to see it. We had one of our conversations in my home and he marveled at the panoramic view of the mountains from my balcony.

Kamča decided there would be no traditional funeral. She knew Michal hated the thought of lying in a casket in front of people with music playing and at the end being conveyed into the crematorium for all to see. With her sons and close family, they climbed up Michal's beloved Lysá hora and held a small service for him there.

She also chose one of his favorite sites in the mountains for the wake on August 23rd. It's an outdoor restaurant with a scenic, heavenly view of the nearby ridge, and the weather that day was beautiful, not a cloud in the sky. The turnout was incredible, maybe a hundred people took off work on a Wednesday to be there.

Štefais introduced me to Jonáš. We talked for a bit about Bosnia and Montenegro. I also talked to Alča, a lovely lady, very spirited and animated, but on that day, she carried the sadness of the occasion with her. The same was evident in the face of Michal's mother Helena. She sat quietly next to his father Jiří, who did most of the talking for them.

I knew some of the people there, like Silvie Milotová, who managed Michal's physical therapy. The last time I saw her was the day after he and I had our first conversation. Silvie and I agreed back then that he was in remarkably good shape for someone who had ALS for as long as he did. There was absolutely no indication that he would be gone less than five months later.

Everyone I talked to was surprised about how fast it all happened. Since Michal's downward spiral coincided with the new drug he was taking, it was fair to ask about a connection there. And then, not even a month after his death, the scientific-medical community was ablaze with news that a woman in Australia had undergone surgery for a lesion on her brain that turned out to be a worm from an animal-borne parasite. The professionals did not think something like that was possible. Now they do.

One of the last people I met was Mirek. His clothes and ball cap gave him away as the guy who first got Michal interested in skateboarding. We sat together in the grass, talking about their youth. He also smelled of grass, which probably explains why he kept on the periphery most of the time, but I think his buddy would be happy knowing he took a toke or two in his honor.

Kamča made a short speech thanking everyone who helped her through these difficult days. Her boys, who mingled with other children in the crowd, were the best she could hope for. Fighting back the tears, she spoke of losing not just her husband, but her best friend. Already she misses Miša, as she always called him, more than she could ever imagine.

As I was leaving late in the afternoon, I noticed there was something unusual about the sun. It was flashing brightly in the clear blue sky, but with no glare at all. You could behold it and the mountains in a kind of wondrous calm, as if both were in perfect harmony that day. This was no farewell to Michal. He's still there, as he always was and always will be.